Edited by R B Heath

TRADE
WINDS

Poetry in English from different cultures

Chinese
Indian
Pakistani
African
Caribbean

Longman

Contents

Introduction

Chinese Poetry
Chung Tzu   *The Book of Songs*   page 14
The Sharp Shares   *The Book of Songs*   16
The Joy of Fishes   *Chuang Tzu*   17
Two Kings and No-Form   *Chuang Tzu*   19
Truthful Words Are Not Beautiful   *Lao Tzu*   21
Fame or Self: Which Matters More?   *Lao Tzu*   22
Taking Leave of a Friend   *Li Po*   23
Question and Answer Among the Mountains   *Li Po*   23
Drinking with a Recluse Among the Mountains   *Li Po*   24
The Ballad of Mulan   *Anonymous (trans. Arthur Waley)*   26
The Painting of an Eagle   *Tu Fu*   29
Jade Flower Palace   *Tu Fu*   30
The Red Cockatoo   *Po Chü-I*   32
Lazy Man's Song   *Po Chü-I*   33
To the Tune of 'A Sprig of Plum Blossom'   *Li Ch'ing Ch'ao*   34
To the Tune of 'Spring at Wu-Ling'   *Li Ch'ing Ch'ao*   35
Dead Water   *Wen Yi-Tuo*   36
The Night Song   *Wen Yi-Tuo*   37
'Iron Virgin'   *Kuo Mo-Jo*   38
Old Mother Blinds Her Own Son   *Yüan Shui-P'ai*   39

Indian Poetry
What She Said   *Okkūr Mācātti*   42
What Her Girl-friend Said to Her   *Okkūr Mācātti*   42
The Long Night Is Before Me   *Rabindranath Tagore*   44
The Further Bank   *Rabindranath Tagore*   45
The Tiger and the Deer   *Aurobindo Ghose*   47
Village Song   *Sarojini Naidu*   48
The Pardah Nashin   *Sarojini Naidu*   49
Obituary   *A. K. Ramanujan*   51
Breaded Fish   *A. K. Ramanujan*   54
The Striders   *A. K. Ramanujan*   55
Insomnia   *Shiv K. Kumar*   56

Poverty Poems – 2   *Nissim Ezekiel*   58
Night of the Scorpion   *Nissim Ezekiel*   59
Again, One Day, Walking by the River   *Jayant Mahapatra*   61
An Introduction   *Kamala Das*   62
The House-Builders   *Kamala Das*   64
Gone Away   *Dom Moraes*   66
At Seven O'clock   *Dom Moraes*   68
I Was That Woman   *Debjani Chatterjee*   69

Pakistani Poetry

Address to the Saki   *Mohammed Iqbāl*   74
Beyond the Stars   *Mohammed Iqbāl*   76
A Prison Nightfall   *Faiz Ahmad Faiz*   77
Do Not Ask of Me, My Love   *Faiz Ahmad Faiz*   78
Freedom's Dawn   *Faiz Ahmad Faiz*   80
Dust Storm   *Nazir Ahmad Shaikh*   82
A Speculation   *Shahid Hosain*   84
Across the Indus   *Shahid Hosain*   86
Sacrifice   *Taufiq Rafat*   88
I Am Glad To Be Up and About   *Raufiq Rafat*   90
Men in Moonlight   *M. K. Hameed*   91
Gold Spot Glow   *M. K. Hameed*   93
A Note on the Existence of God   *Zulfikar Ghose*   94
The Picnic in Jammu   *Zulfikar Ghose*   95
In the Desert   *Zulfikar Ghose*   96
Funeral at the Traffic Lights   *Adrian Hussain*   99

African Poetry

Love Song   *traditional from the Amharic*   102
The Magnificent Bull   *traditional from the Dinka*   104
In Praise of the Blacksmith   *traditional from the Shona*   105
Is It Surprising My Dear...   *Léopold Sédar Senghor*   106
Long, Long Have You Held Between Your Hands...   *Léopold Sédar Senghor*   108
African Poem   *Agostinho Neto*   109
February   *Agostinho Neto*   110
Vultures   *Chinua Achebe*   113
Refugee Mother and Child   *Chinua Achebe*   116
Modern Cookery   *Okot p'Bitek*   117
Modern Girl   *Okot p'Bitek*   120
Parachute Men Say   *Lenrie Peters*   122

You Talk to Me of 'Self'   *Lenrie Peters*   125
Agbor Dancer   *John Pepper Clark*   126
Incident at the Police Station, Warri   *John Pepper Clark*   128
An Agony   *Joyce Nomafa Sikakane*   130
Daybreak   *Susan Lwanga*   132
Tomatoes   *Yambo Ouologuem*   133
Always a Suspect   *Oswald Mbuyiseni Mtshali*   136
The Sweet Brew at Chitakale   *Jack Mapanje*   137
When This Carnival Finally Closes   *Jack Mapanje*   138
To Mai   *Musaemura Bonas Zimunya*   139

Caribbean Poetry

Jamaican Fisherman   *Philip Sherlock*   142
Pocomania   *Philip Sherlock*   143
This is the Dark Time, My Love   *Martin Carter*   146
Bent   *Martin Carter*   147
Uncle Time   *Dennis Scott*   148
Epitaph   *Dennis Scott*   150
For My Mother   *Lorna Goodison*   151
Limbo   *Edward Kamau Brathwaite*   155
Schooner   *Edward Kamau Brathwaite*   158
Earth is Brown   *Shana Yardan*   160
Love after Love   *Derek Walcott*   163
Endings   *Derek Walcott*   166
Dark August   *Derek Walcott*   168
No Dialects Please   *Merle Collins*   169
Shipmates   *Merle Collins*   172
Waterpot   *Grace Nichols*   174
Two Old Black Men on a Leicester Square Park Bench   *Grace Nichols*   176

Some suggestions for thematic coursework   178

About the poets   180

Glossary   186

Contents by theme

Love
Chung Tzu   14
To the Tune of 'A Sprig of Plum Blossom'   34
To the Tune of 'Spring at Wu-Ling'   35
What She Said   42
What Her Girl-friend Said to Her   42
Do Not Ask of Me, My Love   78
African Poem   109
Schooner   158
Love after Love   163
Shipmates   172

In the country
The Sharp Shares   16
Question and Answer Among the Mountains   23
Drinking with a Recluse Among the Mountains   24
The Further Bank   45
Village Song   48
Night of the Scorpion   59
I Am Glad To Be Up and About   90

Inner law
The Joy of Fishes   17
Two Kings and No-Form   19
Truthful Words Are Not Beautiful   21
Fame or Self: Which Matters More?   22
Address to the Saki   74
Beyond the Stars   76
In the Desert   96
Parachute Men Say   122
Endings   166
Dark August   168

Happiness and peace
The Sharp Shares   16
The Joy of Fishes   17
Question and Answer Among the Mountains   23

Separation
Taking Leave of a Friend   23
The Ballad of Mulan   26
To the Tune of 'A Sprig of Plum Blossom'   34
To the Tune of 'Spring at Wu-Ling'   35
What She Said   42
Gone Away   66
Across the Indus   86
Long, Long Have You Held Between Your Hands   108
Agbor Dancer   126

Aspects of War
The Ballad of Mulan   26
'Iron Virgin'   38
Old Mother Blinds Her Own Son   39
February   110

Predators
The Painting of an Eagle   29
The Tiger and the Deer   47
Tomatoes   133

Death and the passing of time
Jade Flower Palace   30
Obituary   51
Breaded Fish   54
Funeral at the Traffic Lights   99
Uncle Time   148
Endings   166
Two Old Black Men on a Leicester Square Park Bench   176

Imprisonment
The Red Cockatoo   32
A Prison Nightfall   77
To Mai   139

Laziness
Lazy Man's Song   33

Night
The Night Song   37

The Long Night Is Before Me   44
Insomnia   56
Night of the Scorpion   59
Men in Moonlight   91
Pocomania   143

Evil and destructive forces
Dead Water   36
'Iron Virgin'   38
A Speculation   84
Sacrifice   88
Vultures   113
Incident at the Police Station, Warri   128
Always a Suspect   136
When This Carnival Finally Closes   138
This is the Dark Time, My Love   146

Childhood
The Further Bank   45
The Picnic in Jammu   95

Nature
The Tiger and the Deer   47
The Striders   55
Address to the Saki   74
Dust Storm   82
In the Desert   96
The Magnificent Bull   104
Daybreak   132

Poverty and famine
Poverty Poems – 2   58
Gold Spot Glow   93
A Note on the Existence of God   94
Refugee Mother and Child   116
You Talk to Me of 'Self'   125

Position of women in society
The Pardah Nashin   49
An Introduction   62
I Was That Woman   69

Modern Cookery   117
Modern Girl   120
For My Mother   151

Aspects of work
The Sharp Shares   16
The House-Builders   64
The Sweet Brew at Chitakale   137
Jamaican Fisherman   142
Bent   147
For My Mother   151

Town and city life
Again, One Day, Walking by the River   61
Gone Away   66
At Seven O'clock   68
A Speculation   84
Across the Indus   86
A Note on the Existence of God   94

Freedom
Freedom's Dawn   80
Waterpot   174

Change
Is It Surprising My Dear...   106
Modern Cookery   117
Modern Girl   120
An Agony   130
Earth is Brown   160

Slavery
Epitaph   150
Limbo   155
No Dialects Please   169
Shipmates   172
Waterpot   174

Music
Agbor Dancer   126
Limbo   155

Introduction

The poems in this book come from China, India, Pakistan, Africa and the Caribbean. They have been put together to give you an opportunity to read poetry in English from different cultures. It is important, as you read through the poems to ask yourself two questions: first, what feelings and thoughts in the poem do we all share; and second, how is the poem unique because of where it was written?

Reading the poems

Before you begin any of the work, read the poem first. Read it aloud or listen to it being read. Make a few notes. What do you notice about the structure of the poem? Are there any rhyming words? Is it written in free verse or is there a regular pattern of stresses and line lengths?

Now read the poem again. Look up any unfamiliar words and read carefully any notes that accompany the poem. Think about the title as this sometimes gives hints about the meaning or message of the poem or may tell you something of the mood of the poet. What is the setting? What does the setting tell you about this culture? Then think about what the poem is saying and what the poet is feeling.

Discussion

It is probably best if you break into small groups of four or five to discuss the poem. Someone in the group could read the poem aloud. Discuss the notes you have made. Do you agree or disagree on the meaning of the poem? Have you missed something that other people in the group have picked up? Have you enjoyed the poem? Are there any particular words or phrases that are noteworthy? How did the poem make you feel – happy, sad, upset, reflective?

Written work

When you are doing the written work, it is important that you write a first draft. Divide your time in two: half for raw writing and half for revision and editing.

When your first draft is finished hand it to a friend. In return you check your friend's first draft. Read the first draft aloud. Ask your friend about any parts you did not understand, e.g. What are you saying here? What do you mean by this? Point out what you liked about the first draft.

When the draft is returned, it is time to start the editing process. Use a pencil to mark on the draft any thoughts or comments arising from the swapping of drafts. Re-read what you have written and use a different coloured pen to carry out the following: altering words that need changing; getting rid of surplus words; adding words to make sentences more interesting; changing any ideas; correcting spelling and punctuation mistakes; and changing layout and presentation (e.g. Should paragraphs be changed around? Am I happy with the structure of my poem?). Then write the final draft neatly for inclusion in your coursework folder.

A note on translation

The Chinese poems, and a few of the Indian, Pakistani and African poems in this book have been translated into English. These poems were originally written in a different language, and in some cases, a different script. It is important that you are aware of the translation process when you are reading these particular poems. In order to help you understand this, look at the following example.

Here is the Urdu text of a short poem by Faiz Ahmad Faiz.

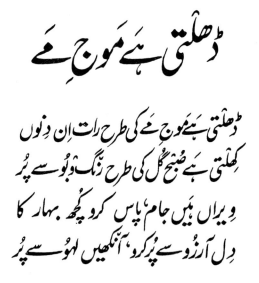

A poem written in a different script is difficult to translate into English without some of its spirit being lost. Translators have tried several ways to retain the rhythm, rhyme, sense and meaning of the original but they are not always successful. One of the methods in use is as follows.

First, the Urdu text is studied very carefully and then each Urdu character is turned into a letter of the Roman alphabet. This is known as transliteration, and the poem on page 10 now looks like this:

Like Flowing Wine

Night at this season comes on like flowing wine;
Dawn unfolds like a rose, all colour and scent.
If dust has filled the cup, pay honour to Spring –
With longing fill your heart, your eyes with fire.

The literal translation is then versified by the translator or a poet working with him or her:

Flows like a Wave of Wine

Night flows these days like a wave of wine,
Dawn opens like a rose full of colour and scent;
If cups are desolate, have some respect for spring:
Fill the heart with desire, the eyes with blood.

For someone not able to read Urdu the effect is something akin to that of watching a butterfly emerge from a chrysalis. On the other hand, readers of Urdu no doubt think of it as the death of the butterfly because the original has been destroyed.

Think about the following: What are the main differences between the transliteration and the versification? What is the total effect of versification? Make your own versification of the transliterated poem, *Like Flowing Wine*.

For Barbara
Who kept the home fires burning

Chinese
Poetry

Chung Tzu

I beg you, Chung Tzu,
Do not break into my house,
Do not force a way through the willows I planted.
It is not that I care for the willows,
Only I fear my father and mother.
I love you, Chung Tzu, dearly –
Oh, but I am afraid, really afraid
Of what my father and mother will say.

I beg you, Chung Tzu,
Do not leap through my wall,
Do not force a way through the mulberries I planted.
It is not that I care for the mulberries,
Only I fear my brothers.
I love you, Chung Tzu, dearly –
Oh, but I am afraid, really afraid
Of what my brothers will say.

I beg you, Chung Tzu,
Do not come through my garden,
Do not force a way through the sandalwood I have planted.
It is not that I care for the sandalwood,
I am afraid of people talking.
I love you, Chung Tzu, dearly,
Only I am afraid, really afraid
Of what they will say.

from *The Book of Songs*

Discussion

This poem and the next one are more than 2000 years old and come from a distant country. How much difference does that make to the way you read them?

1 Who is the speaker in the poem? Do you think the speaker is male or female? Why do you think this?
2 To whom is the speaker talking and why?
3 What is revealed about the speaker's character? Is the speaker sincere about love?
4 Look at the lines and phrases that are repeated in all three stanzas. What does this add to the poem when it is read aloud?

Written work

Is there a future for this couple? Or is it quite hopeless? Bring the situation to a conclusion by either:
a) continuing the poem for another two or three verses, or
b) continuing the story of the pair in prose, or
c) telling a similar story set in modern times.

The Sharp Shares

Swee-swee go the sharp shares
There where they are working in the south acre,
Sowing the many kinds of grain,
Each seed holding a moist germ.
The women come to gaze at us,
They bring round and square baskets
Filled with fine millet,
Wearing finely woven straw hats.
They dig their hoes deep in the earth,
They slice away smartweed and thistle brier.
Where thistle brier and smartweed have grown rotten,
The millet grows to sheer heights.
Rustling of the reaping,
Plumping of fat sheaves,
Piling like a heaped wall,
Shaped like a toothed comb.
A hundred barns open to receive them.
When the hundred barns are brimming over,
The wives and children are at peace.
We sacrifice the yellow black-muzzled bull,
The bull with the crooked horns.
So it will be forever
According to the wisdom of the sages.

from *The Book of Songs*

shares: ploughshares

Discussion

1 In the first line, the poet uses *swee-swee* to describe the sound of the ploughshares. Words which sound like the noise they describe are called *onomatopoeia*. Can you find other examples of onomatopoeia in the poem?
2 The poet also uses *similes* (a comparison of one thing with another using *like* or *as*). Can you find two similes in the poem?
3 Explain in your own words the last two lines of the poem.
4 How would you describe the *mood* of the poem and the poet's attitude towards farming in the village?

Written work

Write you own harvest festival poem.

The Joy of Fishes

Chuang Tzu and Hui Tzu
Were crossing Hao river
By the dam.

Chuang said:
'See how free
The fishes leap and dart:
That is their happiness.'

Hui replied:
'Since you are not a fish
How do you know
What makes fishes happy?'

Chuang said:
'Since you are not I
How can you possibly know
That I do not know
What makes fishes happy?'

Hui argued:
'If I, not being you,
Cannot know what you know
It follows that you
Not being a fish
Cannot know what they know.'

Chuang said:
'Wait a minute!
Let us get back
To the original question.
What you asked me was
"How do you know
What makes fishes happy?"
From the terms of your question
You evidently know I know
What makes fishes happy.

'I know the joy of fishes
In the river
Through my own joy, as I go walking
Along the same river.'

Chuang Tzu
trans. *Thomas Merton*

Written work

1 In your own words, write out the discussion between the two friends.
2 What do you think of Chuang's final answer? Write a paragraph or two
  explaining what you feel about it.

Two Kings and No-Form

The South Sea King was Act-on-Your Hunch.
The North Sea King was Act-in-a-Flash.
The King of the place between them was
No-Form.

Now South Sea King
And North Sea King
Used to go together often
To the land of No-Form:
He treated them well.

So they consulted together
They thought up a good turn,
A pleasant surprise, for No-Form
In token of appreciation.

'Men,' they said, 'have seven openings
For seeing, hearing, eating, breathing,
And so on. But No-Form
Has no openings. Let's make him
a few holes.'
So after that
They put holes in No-Form,
One a day, for seven days.
And when they finished the seventh opening,
Their friend lay dead.

Lao Tan said: 'To organise is to destroy.'

Chuang Tzu
trans. *Thomas Merton*

Discussion

1 What do each of the nicknames tell us about the three kings?
2 Why did the North and South Kings wish to do No-Form a good turn?
3 How did the other Kings re-organise No-Form?
4 'To organise is to destroy.' How is this illustrated in the poem?
5 Can you give examples from your own experience of organisation (even if well-intentioned) that destroyed?

Written work

A *parable* is a short simple story which teaches a moral or religious lesson. Are these two poems by Chuang Tzu forms of parable? What lessons might they be trying to teach? Can you write something similar in verse? Why not try with this story about Aesop?

One day Aesop was sitting by the road when a traveller came along and asked, 'What sort of people live in Athens?'

'Tell me where you came from and the sort of people who live there,' Aesop replied.

The man answered, 'Oh, I come from Argos. The people there are terrible – liars, thieves, quarrelsome, unjust. I'm glad to shake the dust of that city off my feet.'

'I am sorry to tell you,' answered Aesop, 'that you'll find the people of Athens much the same.'

Presently another traveller came by and asked a similar question, and when Aesop enquired where he came from and what sort of people lived there, he replied, 'Oh, I come from Argos, where everybody is friendly. Honour, truth, kindness, virtue, all these things are found among them. I love them all.'

Aesop smiled and said, 'Friend, I am happy to tell you that you'll find the people of Athens much the same.'

Truthful Words Are Not Beautiful

Truthful words are not beautiful.
Beautiful words are not truthful.
Good men do not argue.
Those who argue are not good.
Those who know are not learned.
The learned do not know.

The sage never tries to store things up.
The more he does for others, the more he has.
The more he gives to others, the greater his abundance.
The Tao of heaven is pointed but does no harm.
The Tao of the sage is work without effort.

Lao Tzu
trans. *Gia-fu Feng and Jane English*

Tao: the way

Discussion

1 Is it true that the learned do not know? How can that be? Can you give examples of learned people who did not, or do not, know? Think about the work *know* and what it can mean.
2 Explain lines 7 and 8 in your own words.
3 What comment can you make about these last two lines?

  The Tao of heaven (the way of heaven) is pointed (difficult) but does no harm.
  The Tao of the sage (the way of a wise man) is work without effort.

Fame or Self: Which Matters More?

Fame or self: Which matters more?
Self or wealth: Which is more precious?
Gain or loss: Which is more painful?

He who is attached to things will suffer much.
He who saves will suffer heavy loss.
A contented man is never disappointed.
He who knows when to stop does not find himself in trouble.
He will stay forever safe.

Lao Tzu
trans. *Gia-fu Feng and Jane English*

Written work

1 Supply answers to the questions asked in the first three lines. Give reasons for each answer.
2 Write a paragraph giving your views on any of the statements in the second stanza.
3 In both these poems, Lao Tzu is dealing with important philosophical issues. Choose one of these poems and comment on what he has to say and the way that he chooses to say it.

Taking Leave of a Friend

Blue mountains to the north of the walls,
White river winding about them;
Here we must make separation
And go out through a thousand miles of dead grass,

Mind like a floating wide cloud,
Sunset like the parting of old acquaintances
Who bow over their clasped hands at a distance,
Our horses neigh to each other as we are departing.

Li Po or *Rihaku*
trans. *Ezra Pound*

Question and Answer Among the Mountains

You ask me why I dwell in the green mountain;
I smile and make no reply for my heart is free of care.
As the peach-blossom flows down stream and is gone into the
    unknown,
I have a world apart that is not among men.

Li Po or *Rihaku*
trans. *Robert Kotewall and Norman Smith*

Drinking with a Recluse Among the Mountains

The two of us drink face to face where the mountain blossoms
    open;
Another cup, another cup, again another cup.
I am bemused and long to drowse; depart my friend;
Tomorrow at morn, if you are so minded, clasp your lute and
    come.

Li Po or *Rihaku*
trans. *Robert Kotewall and Norman Smith*

Discussion

1 In what kind of landscape did Li Po choose to live? What do you imagine his life to be like?
2 What question is Li Po asked in *Question and Answer Among the Mountains*? What is his answer? What does he compare himself to? Do all three poems answer this question?

Written work

1 Here is the first line of a four-line Chinese poem:

'The chill snow is heaped against the sunlit windows.'

Write the next three lines to complete it. Compare your poem with those written by other members of your class.
2 Use the following legend and the photograph opposite to write an eight-line poem of two verses about how the panda got its markings.

The Legend of the Panda

According to Chinese legend giant pandas were once completely white. Then one day a young girl died rescuing a panda cub from a leopard. The other pandas gathered to pay their respects, wearing black shaws as a sign of grief. Rubbing away their tears left stains around their eyes from the shawls. Holding their heads in their arms made their noses black and when they touched their ears, they were blackened too. That is how the panda got its black and white markings.

The Ballad of Mulan

Written in northern China during the domination of the Wei Tartars, Sixth Century AD

Click, click, for ever click, click;
Mulan sits at the door and weaves.
Listen, and you will not hear the shuttle's sound,
But only a girl's sobs and sighs.
'Oh, tell me, lady, are you thinking of your love,
Oh, tell me, lady, are you longing for your dear?'
'Oh no, oh no, I am not thinking of my love,
Oh no, oh no, I am not longing for my dear.
But last night I read the battle-roll;
The Khan has ordered a great levy of men.
The battle-roll was written in twelve books,
And in each book stood my father's name.
My father's sons are not grown men,
And of all of my brothers, none is older than me.
Oh let me to the market to buy saddle and horse,
And ride with the soldiers to take my father's place.'
In the eastern market she's bought a gallant horse.
In the western market she's bought saddle and cloth.
In the southern market she's bought snaffle and reins.
In the northern market she's bought a tall whip.
In the morning she stole from her father's and mother's house.
At night she was camping by the Yellow River's side.
She could not hear her father and mother calling to her by her
    name,
But only the voice of the Yellow River as its waters swirled
    through the night.
At dawn they left the River and went on their way;
At dusk they came to the Black Water's side.
She could not hear her father and mother calling to her by her
    name,

She could only hear the muffled voices of foreign horsemen
    riding on the hills of Yen.
A thousand leagues she tramped on the errands of war,
Frontiers and hills she crossed like a bird in flight.
Through the northern air echoed the watchman's tap;
The wintry light gleamed on coats of mail.
The captain had fought a hundred fights, and died;
The warriors in ten years had won their rest.
They went home, they saw the Emperor's face;
The Son of Heaven was seated in the Hall of Light.
The deeds of the brave were recorded in twelve books;
In prizes he gave a hundred thousand cash.
Then spoke the Khan and asked her what she would take.
'Oh, Mulan asks not to be made
    A Counsellor at the Khan's court;
I only beg for a camel that can march
    A thousand leagues a day,
    To take me back to my home.'

When her father and mother heard that she had come,
They went out to the wall and led her back to the house.
When her little sister heard that she had come,
She went to the door and rouged herself afresh.
When her little brother heard that his sister had come,
He sharpened his knife and darted like a flash
Towards the pigs and sheep.
She opened the gate that leads to the eastern tower,
She sat on her bed that stood in the western tower.
She cast aside her heavy soldier's cloak,
And wore again her old-time dress.
She stood at the window and bound her cloudy hair;
She went to the mirror and fastened her yellow combs.
She left the house and met her messmates in the road;
Her messmates were startled out of their wits.
They had marched with her for twelve years of war

And never known that Mulan was a girl.
For the male hare sits with its legs tucked in,
And the female hare is known for her bleary eye;
But set them both scampering side by side,
And who so wise could tell you 'This is he'?

Anonymous
trans. *Arthur Waley*

Discussion

1 What is the poem about? What do the last two lines tell us about our attitudes towards men and women?
2 Does the poet use any word pictures, e.g. metaphors or similes? If so, are these pictures vivid, strong and clear? Do you like the style of the poem or do you think it is too long and wordy?

Written work

1 Write an account of an interview with Mulan, using details from the poem.
2 A year has passed. Is Mulan still happy to be home or does she long for the life of a warrior? Write your own imaginative account as a story or a poem.

The Painting of an Eagle

From pure white silk winds and frost arise.
Look at the eagle painted with so great cunning.
His neck shoots out, he meditates on catching a hare
With the sidelong glance of some barbarian.
Those gleaming silk loops and gold rings can be grasped in the
     hand;
The roof beams are so clear drawn one could enter therein.
Oh, marvellous, if the eagle could strike down a bird,
On the grass a precipitation of feathers and blood!

Tu Fu
trans. *Pu Chiang-Hsing*

Discussion

1 Read the poem once. Then go back and read it again, paying particular attention to the last two lines, which are not part of the description of the painting. What do they add to the poem?
2 How does the poet react to the painting? How can you tell?

Jade Flower Palace

Where the streams wind and the wind is always sighing,
Hoary grey mice scurry among abandoned roof tiles.
No one knows the name of the prince who once owned this
    house.
Standing there, even now, under the hanging cliffs.
In dark rooms ghost-green fires are shining.
Beside the ancient battered road a melancholy stream flows
    downhill.
Then, from the flutes of the forest, come a thousand voices;
The colours of autumn are fresh in the wind and the rain.
Though the virgins have all gone their way to the yellow
    graves,
Why is it that paintings still hang on the walls?
Charioteers of gold chariots – all have gone.
There remain of these ancient days only the stone horses.
Sorrow comes and sits on the spreading grass.
All the while singing, I am overwhelmed with lamentation.
Among these lanes of life disappearing in the distance,
Who can make himself eternal?

Tu Fu
trans. *Pu Chiang-Hsing*

Discussion

1 What had life been like in the Jade Flower Palace? List some of the people who once lived there.
2 What remains of the palace's former glory?
3 Pick out some of the strongest images in the poem and explain them in your own words.

Written work

1 In the last line of the poem, the writer reflects on death: 'Who can make himself eternal?' Write a paragraph showing how the images in the poem support this final line.
2 Jade has always been important to the Chinese. Since ancient times jade has been looked upon as a symbol of certain virtues. Confucius wrote the following about the qualities of jade which seemed to him to be like virtues:

It is soft, smooth and shining – like intelligence.
Its edges seem sharp but do not cut – like justice.
It hangs down to the ground – like humility.
When struck it gives a clear ringing sound – like music.
The strains in it are not hidden and add to its beauty – like truthfulness.

Think about these words and then use them as a basis for an eight-line poem of two stanzas about jade.

The Red Cockatoo

Sent as a present from Annam –
A red cockatoo,
Coloured like the peach-tree blossom,
Speaking with the speech of men.
And they did to it what is always done
To the learned and eloquent.
They took a cage with stout bars
And shut it up inside.

Po Chü-I
trans. *Arthur Waley*

Written work

1 In *The Red Cockatoo* the bird is used as an image. What is it an image of?
  Write down in your own words what you think the poem is about.
2 Write your own piece, in poetry or prose, about a caged animal or bird.

Lazy Man's Song

I could have a job, but I am too lazy to choose it;
I have got land, but am too lazy to farm it.
My house leaks; I am too lazy to mend it.
My clothes are torn; I am too lazy to darn them.
I have got wine, but I am too lazy to drink;
So it's just the same as if my cup were empty.
I have got a lute, but I am too lazy to play;
So it's just the same as if it had no strings.
My family tells me there is no more steamed rice;
I want to cook, but I am too lazy to grind.
My friends and relatives write me long letters;
I should like to read them, but they're such a bother to open.
I have always been told that Hsi Shuh-yeh
Passed his whole life in absolute idleness.
But he played his lute and sometimes worked at his forge;
So even *he* was not so lazy as I.

Po Chü-I
trans. *Arthur Waley*

Discussion

Is the lazy man proud or apologetic about his laziness? Do you feel sympathetic towards him or irritated by him? Why?

Written work

Write your own song of a lazy school pupil.

To the Tune of 'A Sprig of Plum Blossom'

The fragrance of the pink lotus fails, the jade mat hints of
    autumn.
Softly I unfasten my silk cloak
And enter the boat alone.
Who is sending a letter from among the clouds?
When the swan message returns, the balcony is flooded with
    moonlight.
The blossoms drift on, the water flows.
There is the same yearning of the heart,
But it abides in two places.
There is no way to drive away this yearning.
Driven from the eyebrows,
It enters the heart.

Li Ch'ing-Ch'ao
trans. *Robert Payne*

Tune: these lyric poems were to be sung to existing tunes

Driven from the eyebrows: an outward sign of pain and sorrow, i.e. the eyebrows
knit together

To the Tune of 'Spring at Wu-Ling'

The wind stops, earth is fragrant with fallen petals.
At the end of day I am weary to tend my hair;
Things remain, but he is not, and all is nothing.
I try to speak but the tears will flow.

I hear it said that at the Twin Brook the Spring is still fair,
And I, too, long to float in a light boat.
Only I fear that the 'locust boat' at the Twin Brook,
Cannot move with a freight
Of so much grief.

Li Ch'ing Ch'ao
trans. *Robert Kotewall and Norman Smith*

Discussion

Can you tell that these poems were written by a woman? How?

Written work

1 Describe the mood of the poet in as much detail as you can. Give quotations from each poem and from information about the poet on page 180 to support your answer.
2 Write your own poem beginning, 'The wind stops, earth is fragrant with fallen petals...'

Dead Water

Here is a ditch of hopelessly dead water.
No breeze can raise a single ripple on it.
Might as well throw in rusty metal scraps
or even pour left-over food and soup in it.

Perhaps the green on copper will become emeralds.
Perhaps on tin cans peach blossoms will bloom.
Then, let grease weave a layer of silky gauze,
and germs brew patches of colourful spume.

Let the dead water ferment into jade wine
covered with floating pearls of white scum.
Small pearls chuckle and become big pearls,
only to burst as gnats come to steal this rum.

And so this ditch of hopelessly dead water
may still claim a touch of something bright.
And if the frogs cannot bear the silence –
the dead water will croak its song of delight.

Here is a ditch of hopelessly dead water –
a region where beauty can never reside.
Might as well let the devil cultivate it –
and see what sort of world it can provide.

Wen Yi-Tuo
trans. *Kai-Yu Hsu*

Discussion

1 What is the poem about?
2 Is the poem different from other Chinese poems you have looked at? If it is, what makes it so?
3 What unusual or unexpected words are used in the poem? For example, do we expect pearls to 'chuckle'? Comment on the poet's use of language.

Written work

Read the poem again. If you thought that it is about 'a ditch of hopelessly dead water', then think again. Can the ditch be an image for something else as in Po Chü-I's *The Red Cockatoo*? What might it be? Clues are given in the last two lines of the poem and in the notes on the poet on page 180. Now write a short essay explaining what you think the poem is about.

The Night Song

A toad shivered, feeling the chill,
Out of the yellow earth mound crawled a woman.
Beside her no shadow was seen,
And yet the moon was so very bright.

Out of the yellow earth mound crawled a woman,
And yet no crack showed itself in the mound,
Nor was a single earthworm disturbed,
Nor a single thread of a spider web broken.

In the moonlight sat a woman;
She seemed to have quite youthful looks.
Her red skirts were frightful, like blood,
And her hair was draped all over her back.

The woman was wailing, pounding her chest.
And the toad continued to shiver.
A lone rooster crowed in a distant village,
The woman disappeared from the yellow earth mound.

Wen Yi-Tuo
trans. *Kai-Yu Hsu*

Written work

1 Imagine you are able to get close enough to talk to the woman who crawled out of the yellow earth mound. Make up a conversation with her in which you ask her what is going on.
2 Continue the poem. What happened to the woman after she left the yellow earth mound?

'Iron Virgin'

The Iron Virgin was found in Medieval Europe,
A really cruel torture was she.
Her inside was just a box with sharp nails,
But her outside showed the image of Holy Mary.

The Holy Lady was the door of the box,
From behind her breast a spike protruded.
The victim was put inside, and the door, closed,
The long nail thus pierced the victim's chest.

In Manchuria the Japanese had a new invention,
Sharp nails were lined up on the inside of a barrel.
With the victim in it, and both ends sealed,
The barrel was left in the streets to be kicked around.

The torture had no kind looks of the Holy Lady.
But was equipped with such iron breasts as the Virgin's.
The Japanese, they say, just named it Nail Box,
Ah, they surely are good at imitation.

Kuo Mo-Jo
trans. *Kai-Yu Hsu*

Japanese in Manchuria: Manchuria, a region of north eastern China, became a target of Japanese aggression in the late nineteenth and early twentieth centuries, and it was finally taken over by the Japanese in 1932. After the Second World War it was returned to the Chinese.

Discussion

1 What experience is this poem about?
2 List the differences between the Iron Virgin and the Nail Box.
3 'Ah, they surely are good at imitation.' Which *two* things from Medieval Europe were the Japanese of the twentieth century imitating?

Written work

1 The poet states facts, but what is he feeling? What is the poet's attitude towards the things he is describing, and how can you tell?
2 Which of the two poems, *Iron Virgin* and *Dead Water* (page 36) do you prefer? Give your reasons and then go on to write a comparison of the two.

Old Mother Blinds Her Own Son

It's snowing hard,
The river froze.
We finished the nation's war, but now we fight our own
    people.
Conscription would not reach rich men,
It only reached after my son, over twenty years old.

I entreated heaven, heaven did not respond;
I pleaded with the earth, the earth had no power.
I begged other people, but no one sympathised.
I cried my eyes dry, dreading the arrival of dawn
For at dawn my son was to report to the army camp.

While my son was asleep,
And the neighbourhood lay in total silence.
'Ah, my son,
Don't blame your mother for being too cruel,
Don't blame your mother for being too cruel.'

I took needles.
Two steel needles,
And plunged them into my son's eyes.
He screamed and blood spurted out.
'Ah, my son, they don't take a blind man in the army.'

Yüan Shui-P'ai
trans. *Kai-Yu Hsu*

Note: A farmer of the Mei-chia Village was drafted into the army. His mother stabbed his eyes when he was not looking. He lost his sight instantly. (*Wen-hui Daily*, Shanghai, 7th January, 1947)

Written work

1 Give an account in your own words of the experience related here. Do you find this
   a) a folly of a woman who is to be laughed at,
   b) a sad comment on a woman who tried to save her son from a possible death in the army, or
   c) a mixture of both?
   Give reasons for your opinion.
2 Compare this poem with *The Ballad of Mulan* (page 26). How does the attitude to war differ in each poem? In what ways is the ballad similar and in what ways different?

Indian
Poetry

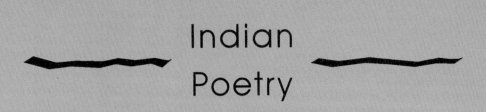

What She Said

The rains, already old,
have brought new leaf upon the fields.
The grass spears are trimmed and blunted
by the deer.

The jasmine creeper is showing its buds
through their delicate calyx
like the laugh of a wildcat.

In jasmine country, it is evening
for the hovering bees,
but look he hasn't come back.

He left me and went in search of wealth.

Okkūr Mācātti
trans. *A. K. Ramanujan*

What Her Girl-friend Said to Her

Come, let's go climb on that jasmine-mantled rock and look
   if it is only the evening cowbells
   of the grass-fed contented herds
   returning with the bulls
   or the bells of his chariot
   driving back through the wet sand of the forest ways,
   his heart full of the triumph of a job well done,
   with young archers driving by his side.

Okkūr Mācātti
trans. *A. K. Ramanujan*

Discussion

Classical Tamil was one of the two great ancient languages of India. Part of its early literature is an anthology called *Kuruntokai*, which contains 400 love poems. These are called *akam* or interior poems. *Akam* poems are written to a very tight plan. This involves five stages of love, each of which can be matched against one of six parts of a day and set in one of five landscapes! For example:

stages of love	parts of day	landscapes
union or marriage	dawn	hill
unfaithfulness	morning	seashore
anxious waiting	noon	forest
patient waiting	afternoon	pasture
lover (or lovers) eloping or journeying for wealth, war or knowledge	evening night	wasteland

The contents of each landscape can be used to provide images which relate to the stages of love, e.g. bees making honey out of jasmine flowers relates to the union of the lovers. Use the information given above to find answers in the poems to the following questions.

What She Said
1 In which landscape is the poem set?
2 Why is the poem matched against evening?
3 What do you think of the simile in the second stanza?
4 Why are the bees hovering and not making honey out of the jasmine flowers?

What Her Girl-friend Said to Her
1 In which landscape is the poem set?
2 What might the cowbells be mistaken for?
3 Do you think the lover may be returning from the same journey mentioned in *What She Said*? Give reasons for your answer.
4 What might a poem set in a wasteland landscape at night be about?

Written work

1 Compare and contrast the two short poems by Li Ch'ing-Ch'ao (pages 34–35) with *What She Said* and *What Her Girl-friend Said*. Which poet do you prefer?
2 Write your own *akam* poem, using the plan given above.

The Long Night Is Before Me

I spent my day on the scorching hot dust of the road.

Now, in the cool of the evening, I knock at the door of the inn. It is deserted and in ruins.

A grim *ashath* tree spreads its hungry clutching roots through the gaping fissures of the walls.

Days have been when wayfarers came here to wash their weary feet.

They spread their mats in the courtyard in the dim light of the early moon, and sat and talked of strange lands.

They woke refreshed in the morning when birds made them glad, and friendly flowers nodded their heads at them from the wayside.

But no lighted lamp awaited me when I came here.

The black smudges of smoke left by many a forgotten evening lamp stare, like blind eyes, from the wall.

Fireflies flit in the bush near the dried-up pond, and bamboo branches fling their shadows in the grass-grown path.

I am the guest of no one at the end of my day.

The long night is before me, and I am tired.

Rabindranath Tagore

Discussion

1 Read the start of the poem from 'I spent my day...' to '...gaping fissures of the walls.' Imagine you are the poet and describe your feelings at finding yourself in this situation.

2 What had happened to the wayfarers of the past to make them wake refreshed in the morning?

3 What did the poet miss on his arrival and what in the ruins reminded him of this?

4 Look at the last two lines. What was the mood of the poet at the end of his day?

Written work

Continue the poem. What happens to the poet, 'the guest of no one', during the night?

The Further Bank

I long to go over there to the further bank of the river,
Where those boats are tied to the bamboo poles in a line;
Where men cross over in their boats in the morning with
    ploughs on their shoulders to till their far-away fields;
Where the cowherds make their lowing cattle swim across the
    riverside pasture;
Whence they all come back home in the evening, leaving the
    jackals to howl in the island overgrown with weeds.
Mother, if you don't mind, I should like to become the
    boatman of the ferry when I am grown up.
They say there are strange pools hidden behind that high
    bank,
Where flocks of wild ducks come when the rains are over, and
    thick reeds grow round the margins where water-birds lay
    their eggs;
Where snipes with their dancing tails stamp their tiny
    footprints upon the clean soft mud;
Where in the evening the tall grasses crested with white
    flowers invite the moonbeam to float upon their waves.
Mother, if you don't mind, I should like to become the
    boatman of the ferryboat when I am grown up.
I shall cross and cross back from bank to bank, and all the boys
    and girls of the village will wonder at me while they are
    bathing.

When the sun climbs the mid sky and morning wears on to
   noon, I shall come running to you, saying,
'Mother, I am hungry!'
When the day is done and the shadows cower under the trees,
   I shall come back in the dusk.
I shall never go away from you into the town to work like
   father.
Mother, if you don't mind, I should like to become the
   boatman of the ferryboat when I am grown up.

Rabindranath Tagore

Discussion

While you are reading *The Further Bank*, try to imagine the scene from the
viewpoint of both the boy and of the poet as observer and recorder.

1 The following lines are repeated three times and so divide the poem into
  three sections: 'Mother, if you don't mind, I should like to become the
  boatman of the ferryboat when I am grown up.'
  The first section deals with traffic across the river at both morning and
  evening. Why is there this kind of movement?
2 The second section looks at the attractions of the opposite bank. What
  are these and what do they tell us about the boy?
3 What, in the final section, is the main reason for the boy wanting to
  become a ferryboatman? What does the boy say that shows he is think-
  ing of himself as being still a child when he is old enough to be a
  ferryboatman?
4 What impression of this part of the river do you get from Tagore's
  description of the scene?

Written work

Imagine you visited the scene described in this poem. Write an account for
a travel or school magazine of the thoughts and feelings arising from your
visit.

The Tiger and the Deer

Brilliant, crouching, slouching, what crept through the green
    heart of the forest,
Gleaming eyes and mighty chest and soft soundless paws of
    grandeur and murder?
The wind slipped through the leaves as if afraid lest its voice
    and the noise of its steps disturb the pitiless Splendour,
Hardly daring to breathe. But the great beast crouched and
    crept, and crept and crouched a last time, noiseless, fatal,
Till suddenly death leaped on the beautiful wild deer as it
    drank
Unsuspecting from the great pool in the forest's coolness and
    shadow,
And it fell and, torn, died remembering its mate left sole in the
    deep woodland, –
Destroyed, the mild harmless beauty by the strong cruel
    beauty in Nature.
But a day may yet come when the tiger crouches and leaps no
    more in the dangerous heart of the forest,
As the mammoth shakes no more the plains of Asia;
Still then shall the beautiful wild deer drink from the coolness
    of great pools in the leaves' shadow.
The mighty perish in their might;
The slain survive the slayer.

Aurobindo Ghose

Discussion

1 What story is being told in this poem?
2 Is this poem a parable? What might it be telling us about Indian life?
3 What lines or descriptive phrases do you find vivid or memorable?
4 Explain clearly and simply the last two lines of the poem.
5 What do you notice about the *sounds* of the poem when it is read aloud?

Village Song

Full are my pitchers and far to carry,
Lone is the way and long.
Why, O why was I tempted to tarry
Lured by the boatmen's song?
Swiftly the shadows of night are falling,
Hear, O hear, is the white crane calling,
Is it the wild owl's cry?
There are no tender moonbeams to light me,
If in the darkness a serpent should bite me,
Or if an evil spirit should smite me,
Ram Re Ram! I shall die.

My brother will murmur, 'Why doth she linger?'
My mother will wait and weep,
Saying, 'O safe may the great gods bring her,
The Jamuna's waters are deep'...
The Jamuna's waters rush by so quickly,
The shadows of evening gather so thickly,
Like black birds in the sky...
O' if the storm breaks, what will betide me?
Safe from the lightning where shall I hide me?
Unless Thou succour my footsteps and guide me,
Ram Re Ram! I shall die.

Sarojini Naidu

Ram Re Ram: an exclamation used by Indian women in moments of fear

Written work

This poem is about a village girl who, having filled her pitchers at the River Jamuna, fails to start her journey home until darkness has fallen. The journey is long, lonely and dark. As she walks the girl expresses her fears of the dangers she may face and her concern for her family who will be worried about her.

1 Write down the *rhyme pattern* of this poem (see page 187 of the glossary). What effect does this pattern have on the reading of the poem?
2 The poem is called *Village Song*, but is it just a village song? Think about the last two lines and the images of darkness and the serpent. If you feel the poem has two levels of meaning, then explain each one.
3 Write your own account, in poetry or prose, of a situation where you have been alone and afraid.

The Pardah Nashin

Her life is a revolving dream
Of languid and sequestered ease;
Her girdles and her fillets gleam
Like changing fires on sunset seas:
Her raiment is like morning mist,
Shot opal, gold and amethyst.

From thieving light of eyes impure,
From coveting sun or wind's caress,
Her days are guarded and secure
Behind her carven lattices:
Like jewels in a turbaned crest,
Like secrets in a lover's breast.

But though no hand unsanctioned dares
Unveil the mysteries of her grace,
Time lifts the curtain unawares,
And Sorrow looks into her face...

Who shall prevent the subtle years,
Or shield a woman's eyes from tears?

Sarojini Naidu

The Pardah Nashin: woman who covers her face under a veil (Urdu)

Discussion

1 Which line in the first stanza suggests that the woman behind the veil is living an unreal life?
2 What does the veil protect her from?
3 What is she not protected from?
4 What is the rhyme pattern of this poem?

Written work

1 Summarise the poem in your own words. (An example of a *summary* is given on page 49 – *Village Song*.)
2 Write a paragraph explaining the poet's attitude to the woman behind the veil.
3 Write your own poem using the rhyme pattern in *The Pardah Nashin*.

Obituary

Father, when he passed on
left dust
on a table full of papers,
left debts and daughters,
a bedwetting grandson
named by chance
after him,

a house that leans
slowly through our growing
years on a bent coconut
tree in the yard.
Being the burning type
he burned properly
at the cremation

as before, easily
and at both ends,
left his eye-coins
in the ashes that didn't
look one bit different,
and some rough half-burned
spinal discs for sons

to pick gingerly
and throw, facing east
as the priest said
where three rivers met
near the railway station;
but no longstanding headstone
with his full name and two dates

to hold in their parentheses
everything he didn't quite
manage to do himself,

like his caesarean birth
in a brahmin ghetto
and his death by heart-
failure in the fruit market.

But someone told me
he got two lines
in an inside column
of Madras newspaper
sold by the kilo
exactly four weeks later
to streethawkers

who sell it in turn
to the small groceries
where I buy salt
coriander
and jaggery
in newspaper cones
that I usually read

for fun, and lately
in the hope of finding
these obituary lines.
And he left us
a changed mother
and more than
one annual ritual.

A. K. Ramanujan

brahmin: a member of the highest caste among the Hindus, having as his chief
duty the study and teaching of the Vedas (sacred books) and the performance of
religious ceremonies

coriander: the ripened dried fruit of the coriander plant, used for flavouring,
especially curries and pickles

jaggery: an unrefined brown sugar made from palm sap

Discussion

1 What has the father left to his sons?
2 What is found in the ashes after the body has been cremated?
3 What does the son hope to find in the newspaper?
4 How old do you think the narrator was at the time of his father's death?

Written work

1 Contrast the last three stanzas of the poem with the first five. What change of mood has taken place?
2 The poet writes about the death in a 'matter-of-fact' way. Does this *add* to the feeling created in the poem? Give reasons for your answers.

Breaded Fish

Specially for me, she had some breaded
fish; even thrust a blunt-headed
smelt into my mouth;

and looked hurt when I could
neither sit nor eat, as a hood
of memory-like a coil on a heath

Opened in my eyes; a dark half-naked
length of woman, dead
on the beach in a yard of cloth,

dry, rolled by the ebb, breaded
by the grained indifference of sand. I headed
for the shore, my heart beating in my mouth.

A. K. Ramanujan

Discussion

1 Describe in your own words what is happening in this poem.
2 In what ways is the dead woman compared to the fish? Use quotes from the poem to support your answer.

The Striders

And search
for certain thin-
stemmed, bubble-eyed water bugs.
See them perch on dry capillary legs
weightless
on the ripple skin
of a stream.

No, not only prophets
walk on water. This bug sits
on a landslide of lights
and drowns eye-
deep
into its tiny strip
of sky.

A. K. Ramanujan

Written work

Write your own poem about a spider or insect. Concentrate on some amazing characteristic, as Ramanujan has done.

Insomnia

My wife snores. My son's dream
fingers have reached the sideboard's
top-shelf for Cadbury.
The sky grins through a handful
of stars while I hold the defiant
pills in my torpid hand.

I'm a double agent. I'll drug
my watch dog to burgle my own house.
I know where my wife's secrets
lie sealed. Each night I hear
the same tattoo in my skull's chamber.

I have counted all the stars
over my terrace. The steel bars in my
neighbour's balcony are twenty-one
and three suburban freight trains rumble past
the rail-crossing between two and four.

Darkness now snaps at the seams.
A hymn floats across the sky
like a bird's warble.

And somewhere down the lane a hand-pump
creaks – the milkman's bottle
jingles at my doorstep.

I must walk through the day's fire
to let another moon demolish me.

Shiv K. Kumar

Discussion

1 What are the pills the speaker is holding and why are they defiant?
2 Do you think this poem is autobiographical? Why?
3 Pick out some similes and metaphors, e.g. 'a hymn floats across the sky like a bird's warble'. Say how they are effective.
4 Explain clearly and simply the last two lines of the poem.

Written work

1 Describe the poem's narrator and show how his personality and character are revealed to us.
2 Have you ever been awake all night, either because of insomnia or illness? Write your own poem about this experience. Like Kumar, include in your poem your thoughts, and what you can see and hear in your neighbourhood.
Compare your poem to Kumar's. Can you tell, from what is described, that one poem is set in Britain, while the other is set in India?

Poverty Poems – 2

I lifted up my eyes
near the railway station
and saw a leper standing
against a poster-ridden wall.

Silent, a beggar,
he did not beg.
Offered a coin
he took it
without a glance at me
nor made the slightest gesture
in acknowledgement. Perhaps
he was dumb and deaf as well.

Dumb and deaf
I walk along,
leper-image sinking in my eyes.
There was another on the platform:
he sang with zest in praise of God
like a happy saint
which perhaps he was . . .
I walk along
leper-music holding up my mind.

Nissim Ezekiel

Discussion

1 What happens in the first two stanzas of this poem? What is the narrator's impression of the first leper?
2 How do his feelings change in the third stanza? What has happened to bring about this change?

Written work

'Dumb and deaf I walk along.' Write a paragraph explaining what the writer means by this line and how it is crucial to the meaning of the poem.

Night of the Scorpion

I remember the night my mother
was stung by a scorpion. Ten hours
of steady rain had driven him
to crawl beneath a sack of rice.
Parting with his poison – flash
of diabolic tail in the dark room –
he risked the rain again.
The peasants came like swarms of flies
and buzzed the name of God a hundred times
to paralyse the Evil One.
With candles and with lanterns
throwing giant scorpion shadows
on the mud-baked walls
they searched for him: he was not found.
They clicked their tongues.
With every movement that the scorpion made
his poison moved in Mother's blood, they said.
May he sit still, they said.
May the sins of your previous birth
be burned away tonight, they said.
May your suffering decrease
the misfortunes of your next birth, they said.
May the sum of evil
balanced in this unreal world
against the sum of good
become diminished by your pain.
May the poison purify your flesh
of desire, and your spirit of ambition,
they said, and they sat around
on the floor with my mother in the centre,
the peace of understanding on each face.
More candles, more lanterns, more neighbours,
more insects, and the endless rain.
My mother, twisted through and through,

groaning on a mat.
My father, sceptic, rationalist,
trying every curse and blessing,
powder, mixture, herb and hybrid.
He even poured a little paraffin
upon the bitten toe and put a match to it.
I watched the flame feeding on my mother.
I watched the holy man perform his rites
to tame the poison with an incantation.
After twenty hours
it lost its sting.

My mother only said
Thank God the scorpion picked on me
and spared my children.

Nissim Ezekiel

Discussion

1 What is the setting for the poem? Where does the action take place?
2 What was the neighbours' cure for mother's pain? Was it medical, religious, scientific?
3 How did the father deal with his wife's illness?
4 How would you describe the mother's reaction to the sting?
5 This poem is written in *free verse* (any sort of verse in which the rules of poetry are thrown to the wind). Compare this poem with *The Pardah Nashin* (page 49). Is the use of free verse a good idea for a poem which tells a story? Why?

Written work

1 Imagine you are the mother. Write about your feelings when
   a) you were stung by the scorpion,
   b) the neighbours tried in their various ways to ease the pain,
   c) your husband tried to help, and
   d) the pain started to disappear after twenty hours. Base your writing on the mood of the poem as you see it.
2 Write your own poem in free verse.

Again, One Day, Walking by the River

The same river, the same sun, the same town.
Out of the corner of my eye
the barge loaded with golden hay
trapped like a leaf in a basin of water.
A tar drum smoulders in front of the judge's house
as four women working rule the hot tar
on to the pitted face of the road.
It is two in the afternoon, and
the heat of yesterday still clings to the old walls
like harsh salt on the skin.
I feel a light wind, so weak and thin
I can't say where it came from.
The day is not yet over. Soon
the mangled lepers will shuffle along, going home,
their helpless looks
drawing fantasies on the town square.
I can't remember hearing anyone
saying he will mourn for me when I am gone.
The tar smoke scatters unnoticed over the water.
I wonder where the day goes.
Even in the bright sun
this was a world I did not know.

Jayant Mahapatra

Discussion

What kind of mood is the poet creating here? What images does he use to establish that mood?

Written work

How many of the senses – sight, hearing, touch, taste and smell – are used for the imagery in this poem? Give examples of each one and explain how the poet has used the senses to give the reader a picture of India.

An Introduction

I don't know politics but I know the names
Of those in power, and can repeat them like
Days of week, or names of months, beginning with
Nehru. I am Indian, very brown, born in
Malabar. I speak three languages, write in
Two, dream in one. Don't write in English, they said,
English is not your mother-tongue. Why not leave
Me alone, critics, friends, visiting cousins,
Every one of you? Why not let me speak in
Any language I like? The language I speak
Becomes mine, its distortions, its queerness
All mine, mine alone. It is half English, half
Indian, funny perhaps, but it is honest,
It is as human as I am human, don't
You see? It voices my joys, my longings, my
Hopes, and it is useful to me as cawing
Is to crows or roaring to the lions, it
Is human speech, the speech of the mind that is
Here and not there, a mind that sees and hears and
Is aware. Not the deaf, blind speech
Of trees in storm or of monsoon clouds or of rain or the
Incoherent muttering of the blazing
Funeral pyre. I was child, and later they
Told me I grew, for I became tall, my limbs
Swelled and one or two places sprouted hair. When
I asked for love, not knowing what else to ask
For, he drew a youth of sixteen into the
Bedroom and closed the door. He did not beat me
But my sad woman-body felt so beaten.
The weight of my breasts and womb crushed me. I shrank
Pitifully. Then...I wore a shirt and my
Brother's trousers, cut my hair short and ignored
My womanliness. Dress in saris, be girl,
Be wife, they said. Be embroiderer, be cook,

Be a quarreller with servants. Fit in. Oh,
Belong, cried the categorizers. Don't sit
On walls or peep in through our lace-draped windows.

Be Amy, or be Kamala. Or better
Still, be Madhavikutty. It is time to
Choose a name, a role. Don't play pretending games.
Don't play at schizophrenia or be a
Nympho. Don't cry embarrassingly loud when
Jilted in love . . . I met a man, loved him. Call
Him not by any name, he is every man
Who wants a woman, just as I am every
Woman who seeks love. In him . . . the hungry haste
Of rivers, in me . . . the oceans' tireless
Waiting. Who are you, I ask each and everyone.
The answer is, it is I. Anywhere and,
Everywhere, I see the one who calls himself
I; in the world, he is tightly-packed like the
Sword in its sheath. It is I who drink lonely
Drinks at twelve, midnight, in hotels of strange towns,
It is I who laugh, it is I who make love
And then feel shame, it is I who die dying
With a rattle in my throat. I am sinner,
I am saint. I am the beloved and the
Betrayed. I have no joys which are not yours, no
Aches which are not yours. I too call myself I.

Kamala Das

Discussion

Look at the way this poem is written. What is the effect of the way the lines often end at an unexpected point of the sentence? Do you like this effect? What does it contribute to the poem as a whole? Read the poem aloud, paying particular attention to the line endings and working out a way to read it that gives due attention to the method of writing without sounding stilted.

Written work

What aspects of Indian society are revealed in *An Introduction*? What does it tell us about the position of women in India? What does it tell us about women everywhere? What does the last sentence mean?

The House-Builders

The cicadas in brambled foliage
Naturally concave. So also these
Men who crawl up the cogged scaffoldings
Building houses for the alien rich.
On some days the hot sky flings at us scraps
Of Telugu songs and we intently
Listen, but we wait in vain for the harsh
Message of the lowly. In merry tunes
Their voices break, but just as little, as
Though the hero's happiness is too big
A burden on their breath, too big a lie
For their throats to swallow, but past sunset
Their jest sounds ribald, their lust seems robust.
Puny, these toy-men of dust, fathers of light
Dust-children, but their hands like the withered boughs
Of some mythic hoodoo tree cast only
Cool shadows and with native grace bestow
Even on unbelievers vast shelters . . .

Kamala Das

cicadas: insects with four wings and long piercing mouthparts. The males produce a very long, shrill noise by means of a pair of drum-like membrances on the sides of the body

cogged: connected or joined together

hoodoo: something that brings bad luck

Discussion

1 Who are the men building houses for?
2 Describe the tunes that can be heard? What does 'the hero's happiness is too big a burden on their breath' mean?
3 What happens 'past sunset'?
4 The poet invents compound words (two words hyphenated so they act as one) to compress meaning or images. What do you think of 'toy-men' and 'dust-children'? What do they add to the poem?

Written work

'The narrator comes from a different background and class to the men that are described.' Agree or disagree, using quotations from the poem to support your view.

Gone Away

My native city rose from sea,
Its littered frontiers wet and dark.
Time came too soon to disembark
And rain like buckshot sprayed my head.
My dreams, I thought, lacked dignity.
So I got drunk and went to bed.

But dreamt of you all night, and felt
More lonely at the break of day
And trod, to brush the dream away,
The misted pavements where rain fell.
There the consumptive beggars knelt,
Voiced with the thin voice of a shell.

The records that those pavements keep,
Bronze relics from the beggar's lung,
Oppress me, fastening my tongue.
Seawhisper in the rocky bay
Derides me, and when I find sleep,
The parakeets shriek that away.

Except in you I have no rest,
For always with you I am safe:
Who now am far, and mime the deaf
Though you call gently as a dove.
Yet each day turns to wander west:
And every journey ends in love.

Dom Moraes

Discussion

1 The poet's 'native city' is Bombay. If you did not know that Bombay was a seaport, which lines in the poem would reveal this to you?
2 From what illness do the beggars suffer? How do the pavements keep a record of this illness?
3 What are the poet's impressions of his native city? How have his emotions shaped his view?
4 Is this a poem about India or is it a love poem?

Written work

Write a piece, in poetry or prose, expressing strong emotion for some place that you know well.

At Seven O'clock

The masseur from Ceylon, whose balding head
Gives him a curious look of tenderness,
Uncurls his long crushed hands above my bed
As though he were about to preach or bless.

His poulterer's fingers pluck my queasy skin,
Shuffle along my side, and reach the thigh.
I note however that he keeps his thin
Fastidious nostrils safely turned away.

But sometimes the antarctic eyes glance down,
And the lids droop to hood a scornful flash:
A deep ironic knowledge of the thin
Or gross (but always ugly) human flesh.

Hernia, goitre and the flowering boil
Lie bare beneath his hands, forever bare.
His fingers touch the skin: they reach the soul
I know him in the morning for a seer.

Within my mind he is reborn as Christ:
For each blind dawn he kneads my prostrate thighs,
Thumps on my buttocks with his fist
And breathes, Arise.

Dom Moraes

Written work

1 What have you learned about the masseur? Write a description of his appearance and character.
2 Describe the situation upon which the poem is based and trace the line of thought that starts with lines 2 and 4 of stanza 1 and ends with stanza 5.

I Was That Woman

At the very beginning of creation
I was dormant, potential, Pandora's box,
A package deal for Adam,
A surprise birthday present
With a time-bomb ticking inside.
He opened me with wonder,
He tasted me with delight.
I was that woman, ashamed and resentful,
Wise yet weak, bold but blushing,
With lowered eyes I walked away from Eden
Without a backward glance, smouldering.
The first rebel, I was the mother of Cain,
And was punished with pain and servitude.
I was that woman, pure and radiant,
Abducted by a demon across the sea;
Banished but dutiful, I bore twin kings,
Till exhausted at last I cried for the earth.
I was that woman outraged by a hundred;
My modesty a never-ending sari,
While righteous husbands watched in silence,
The handling of the property, the strangling of their pride.
I was the woman of mystery and magic
Who sang on the waves and waved my wand
To provide adventures for heroic men on an obstacle course.
I was that beautiful horror with snake-hair
To be slain with a shudder by the brave.
My crime was that I felt for a fellow victim,
Woman-like I wept for fallen Lucifer.
I was that woman, poor and lowly,
Who hid behind a tree and offered
My single garment to the mendicant sage.
I was that woman who tearfully pleaded
And pestered the Compassionate One
To relent and admit me and my kind.

I was that woman who bowed and listened
To Mahavir's message of hope: release
Is mine in a next life – as a man.
I was that woman who destroyed my breast
To fight with men on their own ground.
I was that woman of ill repute
Who washed those feet with repentant tears,
Grateful that he would not lift a stone;
But accepting my untouchable lot.
I was that woman trapped in a brothel,
Who cared not for heaven or hell,
But loved Allah in spite of his masculinity.
I was that woman who roused a nation
And was burnt so many times at so many stakes.
I was the woman at whom the Vedas, the Avesta,
The Bible and the Koran were flung;
Their God was the bogyman
Who kindly sent male prophets
To keep me humble in my place.
I was that woman, silly and rouged,
Of endless chatter, and timeless in dressing,
Whose mind is full-blown and scattered with the wind,
Whose moods mysterious like the tides
Fluctuate with the changing moon.
I was that woman whose nude body inspired
While the sculptor appreciated and chiselled.
I was the woman with soul desecrated
Who typed away from ten to five with two tea-breaks.
I was that woman at the helm of six hundred million,
Who longed to be accepted as simply human:
A real person like others, and not a myth.
I was the woman, neurotic, torn, disowning my sex.
I was the voluptuous, decorative drudge;
I was the creature with will-power raped.
I was that woman. . .

Debjani Chatterjee

Pandora's box: a present which seems valuable but which is in reality a curse (read Pandora's story)

Adam: the first man (Old Testament and Koran)

Eden: see Genesis 2:5–25

Cain: see Genesis 4 (story of Cain and Abel)

horror with snake-hair: Medusa, chief of the Gorgons who had snakes for hair and a face so terrible that all who looked on it turned to stone

Lucifer: the poets say that Satan, before he was driven out of heaven for his pride, was called Lucifer

washed those feet with repentant tears: see Luke 7:36–50

Allah: Arabic name for the Supreme Being

the Vedas: scared books of the Brahmins

the Avesta: the Zoroastrian and Parsee Bible

the Bible: the holy book of the Christians, consisting of the Old and New Testaments; the holy book of the Jews, consisting of the Old Testament only

the Koran: the sacred book of the Muslims, the infallible word of God

Discussion

One way to approach this poem is to look at it as a puzzle. Debjani Chatterjee opens the poem with the introductory phrase 'I was that woman' and then proceeds to introduce us to un-named individual women or groups of women. By doing so, she builds up her own individual picture of womanhood. After you have read the poem several times, try to find answers to the following questions. Individuals in your group may know the answers or you may have to research in the school or public library.

1 Who was a surprise birthday present for Adam?
2 Who was the mother of Cain?
3 Who was the woman abducted across the sea, who gave birth to twin kings?
4 Who was the woman of mystery and magic who sang on the waves and provided adventures for heroic men on an obstacle course?
5 Who hid behind a tree and offered her only garment to a religious person who lived by begging?
6 Who was the Compassionate One and the woman who pleaded with him and pestered him?

7 Who was Mahavir?

8 Who was the woman without a name who washed Christ's feet with her tears and dried them with her hair?

9 Who was the woman at the helm of six hundred million?

10 What was the name of a warlike nation of women who had the right breast cut off to enable them to draw a bow better?

11 Name one woman who roused a nation and was then burnt at the stake.

12 What do the Vedas, the Avesta, the Bible and the Koran have in common?

Written work

1 Describe the picture of womanhood conveyed by the poem.

2 Compare this poem to *An Introduction* (page 62). Which poem do you prefer? Why?

3 In what way could you describe this poem as an *epic* (see glossary, page 186)?

Pakistani
Poetry

Address to the Saki

The caravan of spring has pitched its tent;
The mountain-side is strewn with new-blown flowers.
Red is the tulip in its martyr's shroud,
And eglantines and roses fill the bowers.
The world is hidden in a veil of light,
Blood pulses through the stones and will not rest,
The sky is blue, the breeze is soft and sweet,
Birds flap their wings impatient in the nest.
The mountain stream comes leaping down the slope,
Twisting, winding, stopping, in a rush;
It bounds and slides, its path is always sure,
And then at last emerges with a gush.
It cleaves the rocks that stand upon its way,
It cuts the mountain, sharper than a knife.
Oh Saki, rosy cheeked, this little stream
Has plumbed the deepest mystery of life.
Give me the wine to drink that burns all veils,
The wine by which life's secret is revealed,
The wine whose essence is eternity,
The wine which opens mysteries concealed.
Lift up the curtain, give me power to talk.
And make the sparrow struggle with the hawk.

Mohammed Iqbāl

Saki (or Saqui): originally the cupbearer or page of the Arabs, hence the filler of the spiritual cup, a religious leader or guide

wine: the glass of wine is a familiar image in Persian and traditional Urdu poetry. Here the wine is not literal, it is the mystic wine of the Islamic faith

Discussion

1 Iqbāl introduces the poem (lines 1–8) with lines that praise nature. He uses a number of comparisons. Explain what you think of them as word pictures and what, in your opinion, he is trying to convey by them.
2 Look at lines 9 to 14. How does Iqbāl create the impression of the mountain stream as an unyielding dynamic force? Notice words like 'leaping', 'bounds', 'gush' and 'cleaves'.
3 What do you think is the 'deepest mystery of life'? How has this been solved by the mountain stream? Could it be that the stream's continual action and forward movement means it can overcome all obstacles?

Written work

What do you think of the style of this poem? Have you found it an easy or difficult poem to understand? Why?

Beyond the Stars

Beyond the stars there are still other worlds;
There are other fields to test man's indomitable spirit.

Not devoid of life are these open spaces of heaven;
There are hundreds of other caravans in them as well.

Do not remain contented with this sensible world;
Beyond it there are other gardens and nests as well.

If thou has lost one nest, what then?
There are other places for sighing and wailing as well.

Thou art an eagle; thy business is to soar in the empyrean;
Thou hast other skies in which thou canst range as well.

Be not entangled in this world of days and nights;
Thou hast another time and space as well.

Mohammed Iqbāl

empyrean: the highest heavenly sphere in ancient and medieval theories of the universe

Discussion

Is this poem about people exploring space? Could it be a poem about 'another time and space' within the mind? Find evidence in the poem to support your opinion.

Written work

Put in your own words what you think the poet is saying. Show that you understand not only the meaning of the words but also the feeling and mood of the poem as well.

A Prison Nightfall

Step by step by its twisted stairway
Of constellations, night descends;
Close, as close as a voice that whispers
Tenderness, a breeze drifts by;
Trees of the prison courtyard, exiles
With drooping head, are lost in broidering
Arabesques on the skirt of heaven.

Graciously on that roof's high crest
The moonlight's exquisite fingers gleam;
Star-lustre swallowed into the dust,
Sky-azure blanched into one white glow,
Green nooks filling with deep-blue shadows,
Waveringly, like separation's
Bitterness eddying into the mind.

One thought keeps running in my heart –
Such nectar life is at this instant,
Those who mix the tyrants' poisons
Can never, now or tomorrow, win.
What if they put the candles out
That light love's throne room? let them put out
The moon, then we shall know their power.

Faiz Ahmad Faiz
trans. *V.G. Kiernan*

Discussion

1 What kind of atmosphere is Faiz trying to build up in the first stanza?
2 How has the poet made his description of nightfall seem so effective?
3 Give in your own words the meaning of the last five lines of the third
   stanza.

Do Not Ask of Me, My Love

Do not ask of me, my love,
that love I once had for you.
There was a time when
life was bright and young and blooming,
and your sorrow was much more than
any other pain.
Your beauty gave the spring everlasting youth;
your eyes, yes your eyes were everything,
all else was vain.
While you were mine, I thought, the world was mine.
Though now I know that it was not reality,
that's the way I imagined it to be;
for there are other sorrows in the world than love,
and other pleasures, too.
Woven in silk and satin and brocade,
those dark and brutal curses of countless centuries:
bodies bathed in blood, smeared with dust,
sold from market-place to market-place,
bodies risen from the cauldron of disease
pus dripping from their festering sores –
my eyes must also turn to these.
You're beautiful still, my love
but I am helpless too;
for there are other sorrows in the world than love,
and other pleasures too.
Do not ask of me, my love,
that love I once had for you!

Faiz Ahmad Faiz
trans. *Mahmɔod Jamal*

Discussion

1 Look at lines 1–14. Explain in your own words what the poet is saying in these lines.
2 What happens in the next seven lines? How has the mood of the poem been changed?

Written work

1 The poem closes with the same two lines with which it opened. What effect does this have on the poem? Can you find other poems which use this device?
2 'The poet is turning away from individual love to the love of mankind.' Do you agree or disagree? Support your answer by quoting from the poem.
3 This poem is one of the best-known in Pakistan. Can you suggest why this should be?

Freedom's Dawn

This dawn that's marked and wounded,
this dawn that night has nibbled on –
it's not the dawn we were looking for.
Hoping we would find it somewhere
friends, comrades set out thinking
Somewhere in the desert of the sky
the stars would halt
Somewhere the night's slow waves
would find a shore
Somewhere the ship of our heartaches
comes to rest.

When we set out on youth's mysterious journey
so many hands reached out to lure us back.
From the restless bedrooms in love's palace
so many embraces beckoned, bodies called.
But so much dearer was the face of dawn,
the dress of morning's maiden;
our dreams were stronger than our weariness.

But what is this we hear?
That all the battles have been fought,
that the destination has been reached!
It's all changed, our leaders' struggling zeal;
celebration is the order of the day, mourning forbidden.
Yet anguish of the heart, unfulfilled desire,
nothing is cured by this false dawn.
When did it come and where has it gone?

The lamp still waits for the morning breeze,
the night weighs on us still.
This is not the moment of our freedom.
Keep moving, keep moving!
We have not arrived!

Faiz Ahmad Faiz
trans. *Mahmood Jamal*

Written work

After you have carefully read and understood *Freedom's Dawn*, compare it to *A Prison Nightfall* and *Do Not Ask of Me, My Love*. What do the three poems tell you about Faiz Ahmad Faiz? What can be said about his philosophy, his view of life? Use quotations from the poems to support your view of him.

Dust Storm

The window rattles,
The reed-screen slips,
The ventilators throb,
And ere you get going,
The house is a wilderness of dust.
The sweeping brush and the dusters,
For once their own masters,
Are on the rampage.
The can sits beating the drum;
The winnowing fan goes about dancing.
Mirzā Ghalib has taken a somersault,
He is hanging his head,
And Iqbal is prostrating.
A whirlwind more powerful than others –
An arch fiend –
Reads all the newspapers as it rolls and tosses about.
The crashes and noises have deafened ears;
The mistress calls for her shawl
And the servant brings dāl.
The bush catches one's baggy trousers,
And ere he can disengage them,
He finds his turban gone.
Shaken by the wind.
A brick is dislodged from the parapet;
It falls with a bang on a water-pitcher.
Knocking off its head,
Splashing you with water up to your neck.
When the branches of the trees are wrenched and torn
You feel completely lost.
The cow-dung cakes fly straight to the fireplace.

Nazir Ahmad Shaikh

dāl: pulse – the edible seeds of any of various crops such as peas, beans and lentils

Discussion

1 Read the poem aloud and tap out its rhythm with a pen. Does the rhythm reflect the tumult and confusion of the dust-storm? How does the poet achieve this?
2 How do the contents of the house add to the uproar caused by the storm?
3 How would you describe the tone of the poem?
4 Ghalib and Iqbal are poets who were long dead before this poem was written. How then did they assume the positions indicated in the poem?

Written work

Write humorously about a chaotic event in your life.

A Speculation

(There is a small rural town in the Punjab whose name means, literally, 'Village of the Assassins'.)

This is a mud-infested town
Lost in a blaze of sun throughout the day,
Untroubled by a road, surrounded
By a quiet profusion of fields
Defiant with stake-high corn.

The women work the fields,
Anklet-burdened, stooping to the grain
Or swaying hungrily to the single well:
The water deep, receding from the light.

No children play in the refuse of the lanes,
No voices stir the silent, dragging day;
The air is left
To the warm drone of flies, to the soft plod
Of buffaloes imposing on the dust.

The houses stoop together at one end,
Sackcloth and straw fall at the entrances;
The smoke works, timid and concentric
Within each courtyard, and the beetles click
In the shaking, rotten beams.

There is an absence and a memory here
Soaked into the deep ink-red
Scattered across the walls, speaking from the scars
Grown dark and age-locked in the green trunks
Of the bending, growing trees.

And at night, when the moon abstains,
The men file, white and silent, on the path:

Hurry, intent and silent, and silently
Return just as the town
Surrenders peace before the growing sun.

Then the women return to the grain,
Bending and scything in a busy arc,
Lost in their work, creating
A rhythm and a pause, until one night,
One moonless, manless and remembered night
Across the treacherous, resuming river
And past the high corn the avengers come.

Shahid Hosain

Note: The word *assassin* comes from the name of a secret band of fanatics who were called *hashashin* because they fired up their fanaticism before an attack or massacre by drinking, eating or smoking hashish. Hashish is dried hemp, which under the name of marijuana, is still very much with us today

Discussion

1 How does the title of the poem relate to its content?
2 Why is this poem called a *narrative* poem? What is the narrative about?
3 Tell in your own words the picture you have of this 'mud-infested town'.
4 What picture of Pakistani life does this poem offer?
5 Who are 'avengers' (last line of the poem)?
6 Explain the last three lines of the poem in your own words.

Written work

Write about the women of the village. You may wish to consider the following: their living conditions, their work in the fields or at the well, their fear of retaliation from relatives of those massacred by their husbands.

Across the Indus

How beautiful it seems
That crowded, festering, insistent city,
Dirt, barren heat, the cruel drone of flies,
The sores paraded to indifferent eyes,
The ruined houses leaning to each other
Disgorging naked, unappealing children
Playing their games in self-created filth.
And rising, waiting, casting its heavy mantle,
The suffocating, obliterating dust
Swirling forever in the noisy lanes.

But I have crossed the river
Placing the deep and easy flow of green
Between that life and this.
Clear and toylike in the distance
Quiet, pure and captivating
Lies the city; gracefully the houses
Jostle each other to the river's brink.
So the Indus mirrors
Those dirty shadows like a dream in crystal,
And the ugliness I saw and came away from
Along the placid water flows away.

Shahid Hosain

Note: The Indus rises in south-western Tibet and flows in a south – south-west direction through Jammu, Kashmir and Pakistan to the Arabian Sea. The Indus plain is the most prosperous agricultural region in Pakistan. There are one or two cities on the banks of the Indus but the poet does not name the one he is writing about

Discussion

1 In the first stanza, how is the city described?
2 How does the city change when looked at from a distance on the other side of the river?

Written work

1 How do the moods of the first and second stanzas differ?
2 Compare *Across the Indus* to *Gone Away* on page 66. How are the poems similar (think of theme, style, etc.)? Which poem do you prefer? Why? Which poem is the most effective in presenting a picture of a city that has been left behind?

Sacrifice

As he moves the knife across the neck of the goat
I can feel its point on my throat;
And as the blood geysers from the jugular,
A hot and sticky sweat breaks out on my body.

We are laying the foundation of a friend's house.
After a brief prayer that all who dwell here
May be blessed, we stand in a tight circle
Around the animal to be sacrificed; it has
A civilized and patient look. The glare of the sun,
The heat, and the smell of blood make me dizzy.

The knife is with my friend; it is a necessary
Part of the ritual that it is his hand only
Which should draw the blood. How keenly it cuts!
The movement is a little unsteady, perhaps,
But forgive him, this is his first butchering.
Four calloused hands imprison my jerking legs.

The children are fascinated by the tableau,
And watch in satisfaction the blood flow
Into the hastily dug hole. Two spadefuls of dirt
Will cover me up for ever. A white-bearded man
Chants something holy, and feebly thrusts the pick
Into the virgin ground; the cameras click.

We are not laying the foundations of a house,
But another Dachau.

Taufiq Rafat

Note: Dachau was a Nazi concentration camp at which 32,000 deaths were certi-
fied, besides thousands killed before registration or sent from Dachau for exter-
mination elsewhere. It was infamous for the brutalities that took place there

Discussion

1 What words are used to describe the sacrifice?
2 At which line in the poem does the narrator begin to identify with the goat? How can you tell?
3 What is the children's reaction to the killing of the goat? Does this surprise you? Why?
4 What is the poet saying in the last two lines of the poem?
5 What deeper questions does the poem raise in your mind?

Written work

Write your own piece, in poetry or prose, about the mistreatment of animals by people. Consider what makes the people in your example behave in this way. Is there ever any excuse?

I Am Glad To Be Up and About

I am glad to be up and about this sunny morning,
Walking the raised path between fields,
While all around me are cheerful folks harvesting potatoes.

I am glad to be away from books,
Broadcasts, and the familiar smells,
And the unending pursuit of a livelihood.

Small boys on their way to school
Trail their toes through the stripped soil,
And pounce with joy
Upon the marble-size potatoes left behind by the harvesters,
And with these fill their satchels.

One voice is raised in song,
While the men, hunkering on their heels,
Move up in line like pirates
To uncover the heaps of buried treasure,
And transfer them to baskets.

And girls who should be playing with dolls
Unload the baskets into sacks
Which tonight or tomorrow night
Will be speeding in a groaning truck
To Karachi, a thousand miles away.

And this week or the following week,
Bilious businessmen and irate wives
And their washed and prattling children,
Will sit down at uncounted tables
And hastily devour the potatoes I see
With never a thought for these
Fields, these men, and this sunny morning.

Taufiq Rafat

Discussion

1 Is there a line of thought running through the stanzas? If so, what is it?
2 What is the poet's attitude to the people of Karachi who will eat the potatoes grown in the fields?
3 What is the value of the poem as a statement about farming in rural Pakistan?

Written work

Trace the history of some food items on your table, as the poet has done in this poem. Be sure to include some foods that have come from other countries, e.g. a tin of pineapples. Try to imagine all the people who have been involved in the different work processes.

Men in Moonlight

One feels one can just get up
Stretch one's fingers
And caress it;
Heaven is only ten feet tall
At a time like this,
When the vision is clogged
And perspective
Lopsided with crazy moonlight.
It's scene etched in fancy.
The moonlight is
On a bacchanalian spree,
The moonlight is
On a wild rampage,
The moonlight is
On a sensuous errand;

The moonlight,
Rich, lonely and neglected
Smoulders along rain-beaten window panes,
Drunk on stupor and drugged with
The sight of star-slit skies
It falters, falls and passes out,
Near closed doorways fixed with silence:
Near where
The emblems of honour and dignity,
Kin to greatness and heir to
This one world and the one beyond
Sleep some men,
Turning in creaking cots and
Coughing like choked gutters.

M. K. Hameed

Discussion

This poem is a *personification*. In it the moon is treated as if it were a person, with human attributes and feelings. Find and discuss the ways in which the moon is presented as a person.

Gold Spot Glow

From the stagnant weight
Of the massive grey clouds
A thin long rain fell
With cold unconcern, insistently –
On the creased leaking roof,
On the ancient boltless door,
On the awry mudpainted walls
Of a very old house.
It fell in resolute strings
Of calloused luminous beads
On the sackcloth curtain
Modestly concealing, beneath
The gold spot glow of an oil lamp,
A man, a woman and three children,
Bare to the gleaming ribs,
Crouching in one-tone abstract designs
Around the damp corner, wherein,
Elusively burning firewood
Sends out thick smoke-signals
To the rain-happy world outside.

M. K. Hameed

Discussion

1 In what line does Hameed personify the rain?
2 Why did the family appear to be crouching in 'one-tone abstract designs'?
3 Explain the last line in relation to the interior of the house.

Written work

Write your own carefully observed personification. You could use an aspect of weather, e.g. the wind, snow, or rain.

A Note on the Existence of God

Parking a car in Mall Road, Lahore, once:
a deformed hand, cupped into a begging
bowl, sprang into the window. The hot sun's
reflections were immediately eclipsed.
He lay twisting in the dust, dragging
himself out of postures of pain. Chips
of bone showed through the flesh, his boneless legs
flapped like the behind of a seal.
How hunger deforms! Yet his eyes were real;
this was humanity down to its dregs.
I emerged staring silently at him,
a sure god in his vision in my trim
suit and the perfection of my features.
Locking the car as some gate to heaven,
I turned away from this creature
as surely that other God would also have done,
and walked towards the bank with the proper
gait and dignity of a window-shopper.

Zulfikar Ghose

Discussion

1 What, in your opinion, is the most striking feature of this poem?
2 From your reading of the poem, how do you think the poet himself feels
   about the situation?
3 Why do you think the poet chose this title? What does it mean? How
   does it affect the way you read the poem?

Written work

What dilemma does this poem present us with? Argue the point of view
for or *against* the opinion expressed in lines 15 and 16.

The Picnic in Jammu

Uncle Ayub swung me round and round
till the horizon became a rail
banked high upon the Himalayas.
The trees signalled me past. I whistled,
shut my eyes through tunnels of the air.
The family laughed, watching me puff
out my muscles, healthily aggressive.

This was late summer, before the snows
come to Kashmir, this was picnic time.

Then, uncoupling me from the sky, he
plunged me into the river, himself
a bough with me dangling at its end.
I went purple as a plum. He reared
back and lowered the branch of his arm
to grandma who swallowed me with a kiss.
Laughter peeled away my goosepimples.

This was late summer, before the snows
come to Kashmir, this was picnic time.

After we'd eaten, he aimed grapes at
my mouth. I flung at him the shells of
pomegranates and ran off. He tracked
me down the river-bank. We battled,
melon-rind and apple-core our arms.
'You two!' grandma cried. 'Stop fighting, you'll
tire yourselves to death!' We didn't listen.

This was late summer, before the snows
come to Kashmir and end children's games.

Zulfikar Ghose

Discussion

1 What kind of relationship was there between the boy and his uncle?
2 What metaphors and similes does the poet use? How effective are they in setting the mood of the poem?
3 Why should the two lines after each stanza be repeated? What is the effect of this? Why is the third repetition slightly different?

Written work

'This poem is about the ending of childhood.' Agree or disagree, using quotations from the poem to support your point of view.

In the Desert

When grandma took me to Quetta
the train cut through sugarcane
and maize fields across the Punjab
and entered the Thar desert.

I stood at the window for hours
and watched the sand of the desert
meet the sandy beach of the sky
where the heat-haze broke in waves.

It was the first time that I'd seen
a world in which there seemed
nothing to live for and nothing
with which to keep one alive.

I had a fantasy as children do
of being alone in the desert
and lasting there for no longer
than a drop of water.

I stood at the window for hours
and wanted to know for how long
the world as far as I could see
would continue completely empty.

Now thirty years later when I look back
on that journey through the desert
I feel I am still at the window
searching the horizon for plants.

Zulfikar Ghose

Quetta: also spelled Kwatah, a city in Baluchistan Province, Pakistan

Written work

1 On one level the poet is writing about a train journey through the desert. What kind of experience is the poet writing about on a deeper level?
2 Compose a poem or short story based on *In the Desert* and the picture on page 97.

Funeral at the Traffic Lights

A corpse is passing, stiff in turquoise.
Mourners follow in a broken line.
It is my third corpse in a week.
These are the flowers of April and this is the red neon sign.

More like a sofa than man, woman, hermaphrodite in bright
upholstery. Beyond this, the corpse refuses to be named.
Like many others I simply drive my car.
A keen sun is shining. No one is ashamed.

It could have been anyone, a shady undertaker, a crook,
a waiter, or a wife. Now it lies, its lines jammed tight,
its eyes barbed, its tongue hooked, its tossing
stopped, its silly secrets buried overnight.

The mourners mourn in Arabic. They will carry
the body, as though it were a dead king,
down past the drugstore, through the fish-market, thinking
    maybe
since it died in April, it will dream of spring.

Dust to dust. The traffic sign turns amber.
Tier by tier, the dead are cosy in the rustling loam.
Uncanny parcel, you have been sealed, stamped
and registered, ready for the journey home.

Adrian Hussain

hermaphrodite: a living thing with the organs of both male and female. In this case, it was impossible to say whether the corpse was male or female

Discussion

1 What is your first reaction to the poem?
2 Which details help you to imagine the scene?
3 What is the narrator doing while the funeral passes by? What effect does this have on the poem?
4 What group or groups of words give the best description of the corpse?
5 How do the first three lines set up the mood of the poem? What does this suggest about the narrator's general attitude to death?
6 What do we learn about the mourners?
7 Think about the comparison in the last two lines. How effective is it?
8 What deeper questions does the poem raise in your mind?

Written work

Write your own poem about death. It does not have to be about the death of someone you know. The poem could be about a death you have read about in the newspaper.

African
Poetry

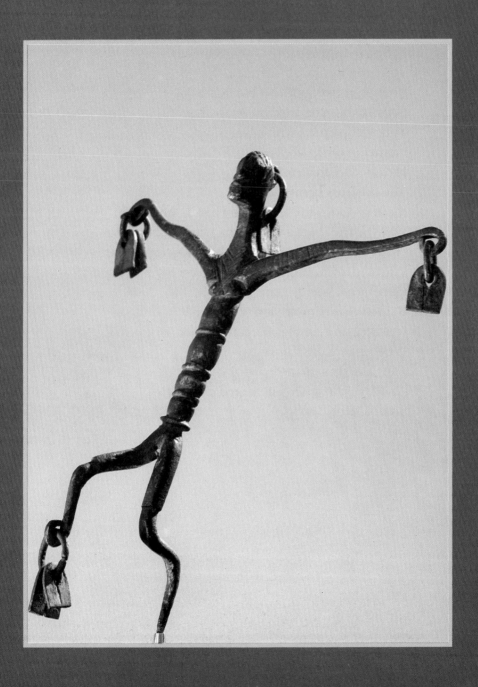

Love Song

You lime of the forest, honey among the rocks,
Lemon of the cloister, grape in the savannah
A hip to be enclosed by one hand;
A thigh round like a piston.
Your back – a manuscript to read hymns from.
Your eye triggerhappy, shoots heroes.
Your gown cobweb – tender,
Your shirt like soothing balm.
Soap? O no, you wash in Arabian scent,
Your calf painted with silver lines.
I dare not touch you!
Hardly dare to look back.
You mistress of my body:
More precious to me than my hand or my foot.
Like the fruit of the valley, the water of paradise.
Flower of the sky; wrought by divine craftsmen;
With muscular thigh she stepped on my heart
Her eternal heel trod me down
But have no compassion with me:
Her breast resembles the finest gold;
When she opens her heart –
The Saviour's image!
And Jerusalem herself, sacred city,
Shouts 'Holy, holy!'

traditional from the Amharic

Written work

The poem opposite is a praise song, part of the oral tradition of poetry in black Africa. Chiefs of the past had their own praise singers, not only for the worship and praise of gods, but also to praise themselves, great warriors and even towns, animals and plants.

Love Song is a song of the Amhara peoples who live in the central highlands of Ethiopia. They are descendants of South Arabians who invaded Ethiopia from the fifth century onwards and brought with them the Christianity of the Byzantine Church – hence the last three lines.

Two more praise songs follow: a song of the Dinka peoples who live in the south of the Sudan and is in praise of a bull (page 104); and a song in praise of a blacksmith and his labour (page 105). It comes from the Shona people who live in the eastern part of Zimbabwe. Shona traditional culture was noted for its excellent ironwork.

1 Write a conversation between the author of the praise song and a friend about the woman who was more precious to him than a hand or a foot.
2 Think about any phrases, lines or ideas in this praise song which you feel are interesting and say how they have given you a picture of the woman being praised.

The Magnificent Bull

My bull is white like the silver fish in the river,
White like the shimmering crane bird on the river bank
White like fresh milk!
His roar is like thunder to the Turkish cannon on the
    steep shore.
My bull is dark like the raincloud in the storm.
He is like summer and winter.
Half of him is dark like the storm cloud
Half of him is light like sunshine.
His back shines like the morning star.
His brow is red like the back of the hornbill.
His forehead is like a flag, calling the people from a distance.
He resembles the rainbow.
I will water him at the river,
With my spear I shall drive my enemies.
Let them water their herds at the well;
The river belongs to me and my bull.
Drink, my bull, from the river; I am here
to guard you with my spear.

traditional from the Dinka

Discussion

1 How does the praise song help you to get a picture of the bull in your mind?
2 Do you find the picture of the bull exaggerated? Why should this be so?

Written work

Write a similar praise song about a favourite pet or a wild animal whose conservation you feel strongly about.

In Praise of the Blacksmith

Today this place is full of noise and jollity.
The guiding spirit that enables my husband to forge makes
    him do wonders.
All those who lack hoes for weeding, come and buy!
Hoes and choppers are here in plenty.
My husband is a craftsman in iron,
Truly a wizard at forging hoes.
Ah, here they are! They have come eager to find hoes.
Ah, the iron itself is aglow, it is molten red with heat,
And the ore is ruddy and incandescent.
My husband is an expert in working iron,
A craftsman who sticks like wax to his trade.
On the day when the urge to forge comes upon him,
The bellows do everything but speak.
The pile of slag rises higher and higher.
Just look at what has been forged,
At the choppers, at the hoes, at the battle axes,
And here at the pile of hatchets,
Then look at the double-bladed knives and the adzes.
Merely to list them all seems like boasting.
As for fowl and goats, they cover my yard.
They all come from the sale of tools and weapons.
Here is where you see me eating at ease with a spoon.

traditional from the Shona

Written work

1 Using quotations from the poems, contrast the picture of the woman
that is created in *Love Song* with that of the man in *In Praise of a Blacksmith*.
2 Write your own praise poem. Before you begin, decide upon the virtues
you are going to praise. You could write about a real person or make up
a 'god' or 'goddess'.

Is It Surprising My Dear...

Is it surprising my dear if my melody has become sombre
If I have laid aside the smooth reed for the khalam and tama
And the green smell of the ricefields for the grumbling of the
    drums?

Listen to the menace of the old men – diviners, cannonade of
    wrath of God.
Ah! perhaps the crimson voice of your dyali will cease for ever.
That is the reason my rhythm has grown so urgent my fingers
    bleed on my khalam.

Perhaps tomorrow my dear I shall fall on an unappeased soil
Full of regret for your setting eyes, and the misty drumbeat of
    the pounding in the mortars back home.
And in the dusk you will be full of regret for the burning voice
    that sang once your dark beauty.

Léopold Sédar Senghor

Note: Is It Surprising My Dear and *Long, Long Have You Held Between Your Hands* are two of the twenty-four poems dedicated by Senghor to his wife. They were published under the title *Chants pour Signare* (Songs for Signare). 'Signare' is the Senegalese version of 'Senhora', the title given to a married woman. Many of these poems sought to portray Africa in the image of a beautiful woman.

khalam: a four-stringed guitar

tama: a small drum carried under the arm

dyali: poet

Discussion

1 What question is the poet asking in the first stanza?
2 What is the effect of contrasting 'the smooth reed' with the 'grumbling of the drums'?
3 How does the sombre mood of the poet affect the kind of musical instruments he plays?
4 Read the poem aloud. Is there any recognisable rhythm?
5 Give reasons why you do or do not feel that the poet is just feeling sorry for himself.

Written work

Senghor suggests that this poem might be accompanied by a *khalam*. Here are other African musical instruments, some of which may be used to accompany poems: balafong, gorong, mbalakh, riti, tabala, flutes. Find out what you can about these from your school and public libraries. The *Encyclopaedia Britannica* would make a good starting point. Write up your findings for your coursework file. How do you think each of these instruments might contribute to the performance of a poem?

Long, Long Have You Held Between Your Hands...

(for khalam)

Long, long have you held between your hands the black face
    of the warrior
Held as if already there fell on it a twilight of death.
From the hill I have seen the sun set in the bays of your eyes
When shall I see again, my country, the pure horizon of your
    face?
When shall I sit down once more at the dark table of your
    breast?
Hidden in the half-darkness, the nest of gentle words.

I shall see other skies and other eyes
I shall drink at the spring of other mouths cooler than lemons
I shall sleep under the roof of other heads of hair in shelter
    from storms.
But every year, when the rum of springtime sets my memory
    ablaze,
I shall be full of regret for my homeland and the rain from your
    eyes on the thirsty savannahs.

Léopold Sédar Senghor
trans. *John Reed and Clive Wake*

Written work

How has 'Africa' been personified in *Long Long Have You Held Between Your Hands*? Use quotations from the poem to support your view.

African Poem

There on the horizon
the fire
and the dark silhouettes of the imbondeiro trees
with their arms raised
in the air the green smell of burnt palm trees

On the road
the line of Bailundo porters
groaning under their loads of crueira

In the room
the sweet sweet-eyed mulatress
retouching her face with rouge and rice-powder
the woman under her many clothes moving her hips
on the bed
the sleepless man thinking
of buying knives and forks to eat with at a table

On the sky the reflections
of the fire
and the silhouettes of the blacks at the drums
with their arms raised
in the air the warm tune of marimbas

On the road the porters
in the room the mulatress
in the bed the sleepless man

The burning coals consuming
consuming with fire
the warm country of the horizons.

Agostinho Neto
trans. *W. S. Merwin*

crueira: maize flour

mulatress: a woman who has one white and one black parent

marimbas: an African musical instrument similar to a large xylophone

Discussion

1 The poem has six stanzas. What happens in each stanza?
2 Why does the poem have *African Poem* as its title?
3 What details help you to imagine the African scenes described?
4 What is meant by the last three lines of the poem?
5 How does the poet feel about Africa?

Written work

Write your own poem about a particular region or country. What details would be important to the impression you are trying to make?

February

It was then the Atlantic
in the course of time
gave back the carcasses of men
swathed in white flowers of foam
and in the victim's boundless hate,
brought on waves of death's congealed blood

And the beaches were smothered by crows and
jackals with a bestial hunger for the battered flesh
on the sands
of the land, scorched by the terror of centuries

enslaved and chained,
of the land called green
which children even now call green for hope.

It was then that the bodies in the sea
swelled up with shame and salt
in the course of time
in blood-stained waters
of desire and weakness.

It was then that in our eyes, fired
now with blood, now with life, now with death,
we buried our dead victoriously
and on the graves made recognition
of the reason men were sacrificed
for love,
for peace,
even while facing death, in the course of time,
in blood-stained waters

And within us
the green land of San Tome
will also be the island of love.

Agostinho Neto
trans. *Margaret Dickinson*

February: It was on 4 February 1961 that the Angolan revolution began

Discussion

1 What is happening in the first three stanzas of the poem? Are the victorious dead buried? Why not?
2 In stanza 4, the poet is projecting into the future. Explain the meaning of this stanza in your own words.

Written work

1 Taking each stanza separately, write about the progression of thought and feeling in this poem.
2 How would this story be presented in a television news bulletin on (a) a station occupied by the revolutionaries and (b) a station run by the Portuguese authorities? Work out a script for each story, including interviews with people you think would help make the events clearer and more informative from each point of view.

Vultures

In the greyness
and drizzle of one despondent
dawn unstirred by harbingers
of sunbreak a vulture
perching high on broken
bone of a dead tree
nestled close to his
mate his smooth
bashed-in head, a pebble
on a stem rooted in
a dump of gross
feathers, inclined affectionately
to hers. Yesterday they picked
the eyes of a swollen
corpse in a water-logged
trench and ate the
things in its bowel. Full
gorged they chose their roost
keeping the hollowed remnant
in easy range of cold
telescopic eyes...

Strange
indeed how love in other
ways so particular
will pick a corner
in that charnel-house
tidy it and coil up there, perhaps
even fall asleep – her face
turned to the wall!
. . . Thus the Commandant at Belsen
Camp going home for
the day with fumes of
human roast clinging
rebelliously to his hairy
nostrils will stop
at the wayside sweet-shop
and pick up a chocolate
for his tender offspring
waiting at home for Daddy's
return . . .
        Praise bounteous
providence if you will
that grants even an ogre
a tiny glow-worm
tenderness encapsulated
in icy caverns of a cruel
heart or else despair
for in the very germ
of that kindred love is
lodged the perpetuity
of evil.

Chinua Achebe

despondent: unhappy due to disappointment

harbingers: something that foreshadows what is to come

Belsen: a Nazi concentration camp inside Germany

providence: divine or superhuman guidance or care

encapsulated: to enclose in a small space as in a capsule

perpetuity: for ever, eternal

Discussion

1 In your own words, explain what is happening in the first twenty-one lines of the poem.
2 How is 'love' described in lines 22 to 29?
3 What is the link between the 'Commandant at Belsen' and the 'vultures'?
4 How many of the senses (sight, hearing, touch, taste and smell) are used for imagery in this poem? Give examples and explain how the poet has used the senses to give the reader a more vivid picture.
5 What two possible ways of thinking does Achebe offer us in the final lines of the poem?

Written work

'In spite of everything I still believe people are really good at heart' – Anne Frank, from *The Diary of Anne Frank*. Anne Frank died in Belsen concentration camp (the camp mentioned in this poem). Do you agree with her statement? Give examples from history, your reading and your own experience to support your point of view.

Refugee Mother and Child

No Madonna and Child could touch
that picture of a mother's tenderness
for a son she soon will have to forget.

The air was heavy with odours
of diarrhoea of unwashed children
with washed-out ribs and dried-up
bottoms struggling in laboured
steps behind blown empty bellies. Most
mothers there had long ceased
to care but not this one; she held
a ghost smile between her teeth
and in her eyes the ghost of a mother's
pride as she combed the rust-coloured
hair left on his skull and then –
singing in her eyes – began carefully
to part it...In another life this
would have been a little daily
act of no consequence before his
breakfast and school; now she
did it like putting flowers
on a tiny grave.

Chinua Achebe

Discussion

1 How do you know that the child is going to die? What phrases does
  Achebe use to tell us this? Why are these phrases so effective?
2 What does the poem tell us of Achebe's thinking and feeling about the
  situation he describes?

Written work

Most of us have seen newsreel coverage of camps of the starving. Does this poem create the same kind of effect? Comment on the similarities and the differences between this poem and a news item describing a similar scene. How does each attract the attention and then create a reaction in the reader or viewer? Be specific.

Modern Cookery

My husband says
He rejects me
Because I do not appreciate
White men's foods,
And that I do not know
How to hold
The spoon and the fork.

He is angry with me
Because I do not know
How to cook
As white women do
And I refuse
To eat chicken
And to drink raw eggs
As white women do.

He says
He is ashamed of me
Because when he opens
The tin of lobster
I feel terribly sick,
Or when he relates
How, when he was in the white man's country
They ate frogs and shells
And tortoise and snakes
My stomach rebels
And throws its contents out
Through my mouth.

He complains endlessly.
He says
Had I been to school
I would have learned
How to use
White men's cooking stoves.

I confess,
I do not deny!
I do not know
How to cook like a white woman.
I cannot use the primus stove.
I do not know
How to light it,
And when it gets blocked
How can I prick it?
The thing roars
Like a male lion.
It frightens me!

They say
It once burst

And the flames burnt
A goat to death!

I really hate
The charcoal stove!
Your hand is always
Charcoal-dirty
And anything you touch
Is blackened;
And your finger nails
Resemble those of the poison woman.
It is so difficult to start.
You wait for the winds
To blow
But whenever you are in a hurry
The winds go off to visit
Their mothers-in-law.

The electric fire kills people
They say
It is lightning,
They say
The white man has trapped
And caught the Rain-Cock
And imprisoned it
In a heavy steel house.

The wonders of the white men
Are many!
They leave me speechless!

Okot p'Bitek

Discussion

1 In about forty words say what *Modern Cookery* is about.
2 Why is the poem called *Modern Cookery*?
3 Is the style conversational and down-to-earth or elevated and literary? How does the style contribute to the general effect of the poem?
4 What is the tone or mood of the poem?
5 What do you think this poem sets out to do? How successful is it?
6 What kind of picture does the speaker in the poem create of her husband?
7 How does the poet suggest that the wife is not used to the ways of the white man?

Written work

1 Argue *for* or *against* the wife's viewpoint.
2 Imagine you are the mother or father of the husband. Write a letter to a friend in which you explain what is happening in your son's marriage. Before you begin, decide whose side you are on: your son's or your daughter's-in-law.

Modern Girl

Ocol is no longer in love with the old type.
He is in love with a modern girl;
The name of the beautiful one
Is Clementine.

Brother, when you see Clementine!
The beautiful one aspires
To look like a white woman;

Her lips are red-hot
Like glowing charcoal,
She resembles the wild cat,
That has dipped its mouth in blood,
Her mouth is like red yaws,
It looks like an open ulcer,
Like the mouth of a fiend!

Tina dusts powder on her face
And it looks so pale;
She resembles a wizard
Getting ready for the midnight dance;

She dusts the ash-dirt all over her face
And when little sweat
Begins to appear on her body
She looks like the guinea fowl!

The smell of carbolic soap
Makes me sick,
And the smell of powder
Provokes the ghosts in my head;
It is then necessary to fetch a goat
From my mother's brother.
The sacrifice over,
The ghost-dance drum must sound,
The ghost be laid,
And my peace restored.

Okot p'Bitek

Discussion

1 How does Clementine try to look like a white woman?
2 In stanza 5, Clementine is said to look like a guinea fowl when sweat streaks the powder on her face. Can you explain why?

3 Is the narrator a woman? What is the narrator's attitude towards Clementine?

Written work

1 In this poem and in *Modern Cookery*, Okot p'Bitek is presenting us with a dilemma faced by some people in the Third World. Should they adopt Western ways wholesale or stick to traditional ways? What do you think? Why?
2 Do you find this poem funny? Write about your reaction to the poem, giving specific examples of the way it made an impression on you.

Parachute Men Say...

Parachute men say
The first jump
Takes the breath away
Feet in the air disturb
Till you get used to it.

Solid ground
Is not where you left it
As you plunge down
Perhaps head first
As you listen to
Your arteries talking
You learn to sustain hope.

Suddenly you are only
Holding an umbrella
In a windy place
As the warm earth
Reaches out to you
Reassures you
The vibrating interim is over.

You try to land
Where green grass yields
And carry your pack
Across the fields

The violent arrival
Puts out the joints
Earth has nowhere to go
You are at the starting point

Jumping across worlds
In condensed time
After the awkward fall
We are always at the starting point.

Lenrie Peters

Discussion

1 What confuses the parachutist on the first jump (stanza 1)?
2 Explain in your own words why 'you learn to sustain hope' (stanza 2).
3 What is it that reassures the parachutist (stanza 3)?
4 Explain in your own words 'Earth has nowhere to go'.
5 What do you think is meant by 'We are always at the starting point.'
  What deeper questions does the poem raise in your mind?

Written work

The following is an account of a first parachute jump:

When my turn came I was thinking hard about how to jump out properly, and not asking myself whether to jump or not. Then the green light went on, the man in front of me shot out; I clutched the sides of the doorway, while the air outside the plane – and in fact the whole of space – seemed to be screeching past. One, two – the despatcher was beside me counting with his arms like a boxing referee – then the order to jump, and then looking fixedly ahead so as not to look down, I wrenched with both arms.

The next half-second – for it could have been no longer – is something which no one who has experienced a first jump can ever forget, or indeed contemplate calmly – nor, I fear, is anyone likely to be able to imagine it from a description. The parachutist jumps from a static atmosphere inside the plane into the slipstream flowing past outside at perhaps 150 to 200 miles an hour, and immediately it seems that a rushing mighty wind or raging torrent has struck one side of his body. I have never felt so helplessly in the power of blind physical forces, completely beyond the control of my own will. To be rolled about and knocked over by waves might feel something like it, if you could imagine the sea about you moving at twice the speed of a racing motorist.

Then suddenly there was a hard tug at my shoulders, and the sensation of being a snowflake in a maelstrom ceased as abruptly as it had begun. The parachute had opened. I looked up and felt inside me a great surging gratitude. I seemed to be suspended snug and safe, as I had lain years before rocking gently in a garden hammock, and the contrast and the relief were so sudden and overwhelming that I still wish they had never ended.

from *Appointment in Crete* by A. M. Rendel

Discuss the prose passage above and *Parachute Men Say* . . . pointing out the similarities and differences between them. Which do you prefer, the prose passage or the poem? Give reasons for your choice.

You Talk to Me of 'Self'

You talk to me of 'self'
– the African self. The inner
workings of a man, his caste
the meaning of his life.

Senghor extols the beauty –
the African beauty. The
chocolate icing and mascara 'selves'
along the ports and river's edge.

Go arrow-flight two hundred miles
and ask for 'self', but
when you find him, send
me word that I may see.

Go into villages, not palaces;
look among goats and sheep
under pyramids of squalor
degradation, the moon's eclipse.

Octogenarian breasts at twenty
enthroned in pools of urine
after child birth, whose future
is not theirs to mould or flirt with mirth.

There is your 'Self' crushed
between the grinding wheel
of ignorance and the centuries;
the blood congealed in the baking sun.

Lenrie Peters

Senghor: Léopold Senghor (see pages 106–108)

Discussion

1 Look at stanza 2. What is Lenrie Peters saying about the poet, Léopold Senghor? In what tone of voice should this be read?
2 Why does Peters say to 'Go arrow-flight two hundred miles' (i.e. into the interior of Africa)? Why would this be necessary to meet the 'real' Africa?
3 Lenrie Peters practises medicine in the Gambia. Do you think that Peters' medical knowledge has influenced his feelings as a poet?

Written work

1 Peters describes Senghor's poetry as containing 'The chocolate icing and mascara "selves" along the ports and river's edges'. Would you agree with this description? Base your response on the two poems by Senghor in this anthology (pages 106 and 108).
2 What does Peters think is the 'real' African self?

Agbor Dancer

See her caught in the throb of a drum
Tippling from hide-brimmed stem
Down lineal veins to ancestral core
Opening out in her supple tan
Limbs like fresh foliage in the sun.

See how entangled in the magic
Maze of music
In trance she treads the intricate
Pattern rippling crest after crest
To meet the green clouds of the forest.

Tremulous beats wake trenchant
In her heart a descant
Tingling quick to her finger tips
And toes virginal habits long
Too atrophied for pen or tongue.

Could I, early sequester'd from my tribe,
Free a lead-tether'd scribe
I should answer her communal call
Lose myself in her warm caress
Intervolving earth, sky and flesh.

John Pepper Clark

Discussion

1 What is the dancer compared to in the first stanza?
2 How does the poet show us that the dancer is at one with her African culture? What lines give evidence of the dancer's African origins?
3 What is the poet saying about himself in the fourth stanza?
4 What words suggest the rhythms of the music?
5 Discuss the rhyme pattern in this poem.

Written work

1 In this poem, the poet is celebrating traditional culture and condemning the effects that foreign culture have had on him. Identify the words that show this contrast between union with traditional culture and separation from it.
2 Compose a poem or story using *Agbor Dancer* and the picture on page 101.

Incident at the Police Station, Warri

(after *The Flagellation of Jesus* by Peiro della Francesca)

Stripped to his penis, the convict at
His lordship's command is shooed out
Of his cell into the square to a bench,
Gleaming with grime in the sun.
'Lie down!' cracks the order, and at that,
Superfluous uniform hands as of an octopus
Grapple the prisoner down, one smart
Sergeant mounting his back. Now with the hiss
And beat of a cobra incensed,
The big stick descends deliberate and
Constant upon the shivering buttocks till
Carbolic water, blood, and tears, wrung
Free in spite of iron will,
Flow in one polluted stream, washing
Society of another individual wrong.
And the smell
Fills the air of the first flagellation with thong:
The scared, curious throng,
Mainly of women and children, twittering
At the sight of a tail shrunken
Between thighs, three very important
Looking persons discussing in one corner,
Perhaps the latest list of promotions or
Prices on the market, and in a car
Parked close by, one gallant and another
Asking the girls to more wine and song.

John Pepper Clark

The Flagellation of Jesus was painted by Piero della Francesca (1410/20–1492) during a visit to Urbino. It is in oils on wood, measures 81 × 51 cm, and is now in the Museo in Urbino. Reproductions may easily be found in art books or as prints. The picture shows the flogging of Jesus taking place in front of Pilate who is on the left. On the right a soldier stands with a raised whip but no violence or suffering is shown. About half the right side of the painting is taken up by three unknown figures who stand like statues in the foreground. They are either ignoring the flogging or are unaware of what is happening behind them. They seem deep in their own thoughts and conversation.

Discussion

1 How is the flogging described?
2 The poem is called an 'incident'. Is this all it is? What is the universal problem being dramatised by John Pepper Clark?

Written work

1 Imagine you are a reporter on a Warri newspaper. Write of this incident, including the headline.
2 Study a reproduction of *The Flagellation of Jesus*. How have the details of the painting been interwoven into the poem? Compare and contrast the painting with the poem. How has linking the painting with the incident at Warri added to the feeling of the poem?

An Agony

My head is heavy, my shoulders shrug,
because despite
all my eyes have seen
my head has said
my heart has felt,
I do not believe
that White, Black and Yellow
cannot talk, walk, eat, kiss and share.

It worries me to think
that only people of my colour
will liberate me.

You mustn't trust a White man
my grandfather used to tell me
when I was a child.
You mustn't think a White man cares for you
my people caution me.
You know when a White man wants to know you?
When you bring him money!

The Indian? He's as black as you.
But, not as poor as you.
He knows his trade – cheating you.
He's happy to lend you money
just forgets to mention
the twenty per cent interest!
Until you have to pay it.

And the Coloured? I ask.
Ag! him, they say.
He doesn't know where he stands,
but, he prefers his skin whitest
and his hair straightest.

And sometimes forgets the second names
of his black and kinky cousins!

I know of Whites, Coloureds and Indians
who are not like that, I say.
But, I'm told they are only a few.
Now, what about you my fellow African.
We are intimidated, they say,
Modimo, we're very very busy, they say,

not losing
our passes,
our birth certificates,
our train tickets,
our rent receipts,
our urban residential permits,
(not to mention our money, our husbands and our lives).

My head is heavy, my shoulders shrug,
because despite
all my eyes have seen
my head has said
my heart felt,
I do not believe
that White, Black and Yellow
cannot talk, walk, eat, kiss and share.

Joyce Nomafa Sikakane

Discussion

1 What stereotypes are presented of the White man, the Indian and the Coloured?
2 Why are the narrator's fellow Africans 'very, very busy'? What does this tell you about life in South Africa?
3 What is the narrator's belief? Why is this belief all the more amazing given the circumstances of the poem?

Daybreak

O dawn
Where do you hide your paints at night
That cool breath, that scent
With which you sweeten the early air?

O dawn
What language do you use
To instruct the birds to sing
Their early songs
And insects to sound
the rhythm of an African heartbeat?

O dawn
Where do you find the good will
To speed the early traffic on its way,
Rouse the cold drunkard
And send your askaris and barking dogs
To chase thieves to their dens?

O dawn
Whose cold breath makes young boys and girls
Glad of a warm sheet,
Enflames the dreams of unmarried ones,
And brings familiar noises
To gladden the hearts of the married.

Susan Lwanga

askari: a soldier or policeman

Written work

What 'ordinary' picture of African life does this poem present?

Tomatoes

People think I'm a cannibal
But you know what people say

People see I've got red gums but who has
White ones
Up the tomatoes

People say there are not so many tourists
Now
But you know
This isn't America and nobody
Has the money

People think it's my fault and are scared
But look
My teeth are white not red
I've not eaten anybody
People are rotten they say I scoff
Baked tourists
Or maybe grilled
Baked or grilled I asked
They didn't say anything just kept looking uneasily at
 my gums
Up the tomatoes

Everyone knows in an agricultural country there's agriculture
Up the vegetables

Everyone knows that vegetables
Well you can't live on the vegetables you grow
And that I'm quite well developed for someone
 underdeveloped
Miserable scum living off the tourists
Down with my teeth

People suddenly surrounded me
Tied me up
Threw me down
At the feet of justice

Cannibal or not cannibal
Answer

Ah you think you're so clever
So proud of yourself

Well we'll see I'm going to settle your account
Have you anything to say
Before you are sentenced to death

I shouted Up the tomatoes

People are rotten and women curious you know
There was one of these in the curious circle
In her rasping voice sort of bubbling like a saucepan
With a hole in it
Shrieked
Slit open his belly
I'm sure father is still inside

There weren't any knives
Naturally enough among the vegetarians
Of the western world
So they got a Gillette blade
And carefully
Slit
Slat
Plop
Slit open my belly

Inside flourishing rows of tomatoes
Watered by streams of palm wine
Up the tomatoes

Yambo Ouologuem
trans. *John Reed* and *Clive Wake*

Discussion

1 Who are the different speakers in the poem?
2 What happens in the poem?
3 In what ways is the poem an exaggeration? Is this humorous? Why?

Written work

1 *Satire* is literature which examines vice and folly and makes them appear ridiculous or contemptible. Show how this poem is satiric.
2 Write your own satiric poem.

Always a Suspect

I get up in the morning
and dress up like a gentleman –
A white shirt a tie and a suit.

I walk into the street
to be met by a man
who tells me to 'produce'.
I show him
the document of my existence
to be scrutinised and given the nod.

Then I enter the foyer of a building
to have my way barred by a commissionaire.
'What do you want?'

I trudge the city pavements
side by side with 'madam'
who shifts her handbag
from my side to the other,
and looks at me with eyes that say
'Ha! Ha! I know who you are;
beneath those fine clothes
ticks the heart of a thief.'

Oswald Mbuyiseni Mtshali

Written work

1 In the poem there are three confrontations. Firstly, the poet is asked to produce his identification pass, secondly he is stopped by the commissionaire, and lastly he is treated as a suspect by madam. What is the poet saying to you by recording these confrontations? What is your response?

2 Have you ever seen anyone being discriminated against because of their colour, or their nationality, or because they are in some way different? What happened and how did you react?

The Sweet Brew at Chitakale

The old woman squats before a clay jar of thobwa
She uncovers the basket lid from the jar and
Stirs attention with a gourdful of the brew.

The customers have all been here: cyclists
In dripping sweat have deposited their coins
In the basket gulping down their share.

Pedestrians on various chores have talked
Before the exchange and then cooled their
Parched throats to their money's worth,

But this bus passenger bellows for a gourdful
From the window, drinks deliberately slowly until
The conductor presses the go-button –

The woman picks up the pieces of her broken
Gourd, and dusting her bottom, again squats
Confronting her brew with a borrowed cup.

Jack Mapanje

thobwa: sweet drink brewed from millet

Discussion

1 Describe the old woman's customers in the second and third stanzas.
2 What is different about her next customer, 'this bus passenger'?
3 What happened when the conductor pressed the go-button?
4 What have you learned about the old woman selling thobwa?

Written work

The language and structure of this poem are deliberately simple. How does this simplicity add to the power of the poem?

When This Carnival Finally Closes

When this frothful carnival finally closes, brother
When your drumming veins dry, these very officers
Will burn the scripts of the praises we sang to you
And shatter the calabashes you drank from. Your
Charms, these drums, and the effigies blazing will
Become the accomplices to your lie-achieved world!
Your bamboo hut on the beach they'll make a bonfire
Under the cover of giving their hero a true traditional
Burial, though in truth to rid themselves of another
Deadly spirit that might otherwise have haunted them,
And at the wake new mask dancers will quickly leap
Into the arena dancing to tighter skins, boasting
Other clans of calabashes as the undertakers jest:
What did he think he would become, a God? The devil!

Jack Mapanje

Discussion

1 Froth is to be found on beer. What then does 'frothful' suggest about the carnival, i.e. the way the government rules?
2 The drummer represents the supporters of the government, who praise and encourage mis-rule. What evidence of this is there in the first six lines?
3 Who are 'these very officers' who will carry out the destruction?
4 Who are the 'new mask dancers' who 'will quickly leap into the arena dancing to tighter skins' (i.e. drums)?
5 What warning is the poet giving to the drummer?

Written work

Of Chameleons and Gods, the collection of Mapanje's poems from which *When This Carnival Finally Closes* was taken, was banned by the Malawi government after he was arrested and imprisoned. If you believe in censorship then argue for it, using this poem as an example of written material that might be harmful to a government. If you are against censorship, argue that the poem should be discussed in public where balanced views can be aired and the poem receive fair criticism.

To Mai

(from Prison Letters)

Dear Mai,
as long as I can still cough and spit
as long as I can still hold this pen
I am alive, Mai.
I hope you are well also.
Please do not let your mind fill with darkness
do not gnaw your heart away with grief
I am alive, Mai,
it will be over before long.

Calm your heart, mother,
do not trouble yourself
that you cannot come to see your lost son.
I am not in the leopard's mouth
as you said in your last letter.

You came into my face last night,
so comforting you were
that I awoke with a feeling
that I should come to your hut to say
an early 'Morning, Mai.'

Please, tell little Ruth
to stop crying. Poor child,
What does she know?
A pity she should think I am dead.
Baba shouldn't have said it so straight
in her presence.
I am glad you have a comforter
in the Reverend's wife. My friend, her son,
is still in indefinite detention. So,
as the song goes, 'It's not I alone
who has trouble.'

I long for pumpkins
cooked in the same clay-pot with round nuts.
Preserve me some, Mai. Greetings to all the small ones.
I am your puking child,
Musaemura.

Musaemura Bonas Zimunya

Prison Letters: Zimunya was imprisoned by the white minority government in Zimbabwe when he took part in the liberation struggle

Written work

1 Write a character sketch of the poet based on evidence in the poem.
2 Do you think this is a political poem? Why or why not?
3 Here is a stanza from *To Althea from Prison* by Richard Lovelace (1618–1658).

> Stone walls do not a prison make,
>   Nor iron bars a cage;
> Minds innocent and quiet take
>   That for an hermitage;
> If I have freedom in my love,
>   And in my soul am free;
> Angels alone that soar above,
>   Enjoy such liberty.

Compare and contrast this stanza with the first two stanzas of *To Mai*. In what ways are they similar and what ways are they different?
4 An *epistle* is a poem in the form of a letter. Write your own epistle, perhaps to a friend you have not seen for a long time.

Caribbean
Poetry

Jamaican Fisherman

Across the sand I saw a black man stride
To fetch his fishing gear and broken things,
And silently that splendid body cried
Its proud descent from ancient chiefs and kings.
Across the sand I saw him naked stride;
Sang his black body in the sun's white light
The velvet coolness of dark forests wide,
The blackness of the jungle's starless night.
He stood beside the old canoe which lay
Upon the beach, swept up within his arms
The broken nets and careless lounged away
Towards his wretched hut. . .
Nor knew how fiercely spoke his body then
Of ancient wealth and savage regal men.

Philip Sherlock

Written work

Write on the following theme: 'Even though this poem is called *Jamaican Fisherman*, it is really a poem about Africa.'

Pocomania

Long Mountain, rise,
Lift you' shoulder, blot the moon.
Black the stars, hide the skies,
Long Mountain, rise, lift you' shoulder high.

Black of skin and white of gown
Black of night and candle light
White against the black of trees
And altar white against the gloom,
Black of mountain high up there
Long Mountain, rise,
Lift you' shoulder, blot the moon,
Black the stars, black the sky.

Africa among the trees
Asia with her mysteries
Weaving white in flowing gown
Black Long Mountain looking down
Sees the shepherd and his flock
Dance and sing and wisdom mock,
Dance and sing and falls away
All the civilized today
Dance and sing and fears let loose;
Here the ancient gods that choose
Man for victim, man for hate
Man for sacrifice to fate
Hate and fear and madness black
Dance before the altar white
Comes the circle closer still
Shepherd weave your pattern old
Africa among the trees
Asia with her mysteries.

Black of night and white of gown
White of altar, black of trees
'Swing de circle wide again
Fall and cry me sister now
Let de spirit come again
Fling away de flesh an' bone
Let de spirit have a home.'

Grunting low and in the dark
White of gown and circling dance
Gone today and all control
Now the dead are in control
Power of the past returns
Africa among the trees
Asia with her mysteries.

Black the stars, hide the sky
Lift you' shoulder, blot the moon.
Long Mountain, rise.

Philip Sherlock

Long Mountain: a long, low mountain just outside Kingston, Jamaica

Pocomania: a cult (believers in religious worship with its special customs and ceremonies) that mixes revivalism (renewed religious fervour) with an ancient belief that the spirits of ancestors can be called up to possess the body. The leader is called a Shepherd

Discussion

1 How should this poem be read aloud?
2 What is the setting for the poem? Where does the action take place? Does the language used add to the atmosphere of the description?
3 What is the pattern or plan for the rhymes in stanza 3?
4 Tap out the rhythm of stanza 3 with a pencil. Now do the same with the following:

> Round about the cauldron go;
> In the poisoned entrails throw,
> Toad that under cold stone
> Days and nights has thirty one
> Swelter'd venom sleeping got
> Boil thou first i' the charmed pot.
>
> . . . .
>
> Fillet of a fenny snake,
> In the cauldron boil and bake;
> Eye of newt and toe of frog,
> Wool of bat and tongue of dog,
> Adder's fork and blind-worm's sting,
> Lizard's leg and howlet's wing,
> For a charm of powerful trouble;
> Fire burn and cauldron bubble.

What comments do you have to make on the chants of Shakespeare's witches and Sherlock's stanza 3?

Written work

Imagine you are a reporter for the *Jamaica Free Press*. Write an account, with headlines, of what is going on late at night on Long Mountain. Include an interview with someone who is practising the cult of Pocomania.

This is the Dark Time, My Love

This is the dark time, my love
all around the land brown beetles crawl about.
The shining sun is hidden in the sky.
Red flowers bend their heads in awful sorrow.

This is the dark time, my love.
It is the season of oppression, dark metal, and tears.
It is the festival of guns, the carnival of misery.
Everywhere the faces of men are strained and anxious.

Who comes walking in the dark night time?
Whose boot of steel tramps down the slender grass?
It is the man of death, my love, the stranger invader
watching you sleep and aiming at your dream.

Martin Carter

This is the Dark Time, My Love: the poet was active in the nationalist movement in Guyana. This poem was written while he was in prison

Discussion

1 Why do you think the poet gave his poem this particular title?
2 What picture do you get of life in Guyana at this time?
3 Explain the last two lines of the poem. Is the person addressed 'physically' asleep or not?
4 What picture of the poet have you built up? How does knowing he wrote this poem in prison affect your view of him?

Written work

Compare this poem to *When This Carnival Finally Closes* on page 138. Which do you think is the most effective 'protest' poem? Why?

Bent

On the street, the sun
rages. The bent back of
an old woman resurrects
the brimmed bucket of this world's
light and unsupportable
agony. A damage of years.

Her bent back, time's bad
step, and the creeping out
is ash, is the crushed cloud
of an incredible want.

The last time I saw her
she was far more truthful
than the damage of the years
carried on her back. The
sky, blue and ever,
imitates her. Bent.

Martin Carter

Written work

Write on the following theme: 'The old woman in this poem is a symbol for all humanity.'

Uncle Time

Uncle Time is a ole, ole man. . .
All year long 'im wash 'im foot in de sea,
long, lazy years on de wet san'
an' shake de coconut tree dem
quiet-like wid 'im sea-win' laughter,
scraping away de lan'. . .

Uncle Time is a spider-man, cunnin' an cool,
him tell yu: watch de hill an' yu si mi.
Huhn! Fe yu yi no quick enough fe si
how 'im move like mongoose; man yu tink 'im fool?

Me Uncle Time smile black as sorrow;
'im voice is sof', as bamboo leaf
but Lawd, me Uncle cruel.
When 'im play in de street
wid yu woman – watch 'im! By tomorrow
she dry as cane-fire, bitter as cassava;
an' when 'im teach yu son, long after
yu walk wid stranger, an yu bread is grief.
Watch how 'im spin web roun' yu house, an' creep
inside; an' when 'im touch yu, weep. . .

Dennis Scott

dem: tnem

si mi: see me

yu yi: your eye

fe si: to see

cassava: a tropical plant with starchy roots from which tapioca is obtained

Discussion

1 Who is the speaker? Is it the poet himself or a character created by the poet?
2 To whom do you think the speaker is talking?
3 Find similes in the poem that relate to either the Caribbean environment or its folklore.
4 What can Uncle Time do to people?
5 This poem is not written in 'standard' English. It is written in *dialect*, a distinctive regional variation of the language. Do you think the poem gains or loses by being written in dialect?
6 In this poem, Uncle Time has been personified. How many human feelings and actions has Uncle Time been given?

Written work

1 Write your own poem in dialect.
2 In Jamaica the spider-man (or Anansi) is a popular mythical figure about whom many stories are told. See if you can find out more about Anansi and relate one of his stories in poetry or prose.

Epitaph

They hanged him on a clement morning, swung
between the falling sunlight and the women's
breathing, like a black apostrophe to pain.
All morning while the children hushed
their hopscotch joy and the cane kept growing
he hung there sweet and low.
        At least that's how
they tell it. It was long ago
and what can we recall of a dead slave or two
except that when we punctuate our island tale
they swing like sighs across the brutal
sentences, and anger pauses
till they pass away.

Dennis Scott

Discussion

1 What experience is this poem about?
2 How good is the imagery, e.g. 'like a black apostrophe to pain'? How
  suitable is it for the poet's purpose? Show how this simile is extended
  throughout the poem.

Written work

Explain in your own words what you think the poet was feeling when he
wrote this poem.

For My Mother

(May I Inherit Half Her Strength)

my mother loved my father
I write this as an absolute
in this my thirtieth year
the year to discard absolutes

he appeared, her fate disguised,
as a sunday player in a cricket match,
he had ridden from a country
one hundred miles south of hers.

She tells me he dressed the part,
visiting dandy, maroon blazer
cream serge pants, seam like razor,
and the beret and the two-tone shoes.

My father stopped to speak to her sister,
till he looked and saw her by the oleander,
sure in the kingdom of my blue-eyed grandmother.
He never played the cricket match that day.

He wooed her with words and he won her.
He had nothing but words to woo her,
On a visit to distant Kingston he wrote,

'I stood on the corner of King Street and looked,
and not one woman in that town was lovely as you'.

My mother was a child of the petit bourgeoisie
studying to be a teacher, she oiled her hands
to hold pens.
My father barely knew his father, his mother died young,
he was a boy who grew with his granny.

My mother's trousseau came by steamer through the snows of
    Montreal
where her sister Albertha of the cheekbones and the
perennial Rose, combed Jewlit backstreets with French-
turned names for Doris' wedding things.

Such a wedding Harvey River, Hanover, had never seen
Who anywhere had seen a veil fifteen chantilly yards long?
and a crepe de chine dress with inlets of silk godettes
and a neck-line clasped with jewelled pins!

And on her wedding day she wept. For it was a brazen bride in
    those days
who smiled.
and her bouquet looked for the world like a sheaf of wheat
against the unknown of her belly,
a sheaf of wheat backed by maidenhair fern, representing
    Harvey River
her face washed by something other than river water.

My father made one assertive move, he took the imported
    cherub down
from the height of the cake and dropped it in the soft territory
between her breasts . . . and she cried.

When I came to know my mother many years later, I knew her
    as the figure
who sat at the first thing I learned to read: 'SINGER', and she
    breast-fed
my brother while she sewed; and she taught us to read while
    she sewed and
she sat in judgement over all our disputes as she sewed.

She could work miracles, she would make a garment from a
    square of cloth

in a span that defied time. Or feed twenty people on a stew
    made from
fallen-from-the-head cabbage leaves and a carrot and a cho-
    cho and a palmful
of meat.

And she rose early and sent us clean into the world and she
    went to bed in
the dark, for my father came in always last.

There is a place somewhere where my mother never took the
    younger ones
a country where my father with the always smile
my father whom all women loved, who had the perpetual
    quality of wonder
given only to a child . . . hurt his bride.

Even at his death there was this 'Friend' who stood by her
    side,
but my mother is adamant that that has no place in the
    memory of
my father.

When he died, she sewed dark dresses for the women among
    us
and she summoned that walk, straight-backed, that she gave
    to us
and buried him dry-eyed.

Just that morning, weeks after
she stood delivering bananas from their skin
singing in that flat hill country voice

she fell down a note to the realization that she did
not have to be brave, just this once
and she cried.

For her hands grown coarse with raising nine children
for her body for twenty years permanently fat
for the time she pawned her machine for my sister's
Senior Cambridge fees
and for the pain she bore with the eyes of a queen

and she cried also because she loved him.

Lorna Goodison

petit bourgeoisie: middle classes

chantilly: a fine lace named after the French town where it was first made

crepe de chine: crepe from China – a light, crinkled fabric originally made of silk

godettes: in the 1930s a fashion in which a triangular piece of fabric known as a godet was added to a sleeve or skirt to give fullness or flare

SINGER: a make of sewing machine

Discussion

1 How do you know that the poet's parents come from different back-grounds? Pick out the words and phrases in the poem that show this.
2 How did the father 'hurt his bride'?
3 What picture of the mother have you built up? What picture of the father?
4 What is the importance of the sub-title?

Written work

1 Describe the picture of Caribbean life that is presented in this poem.
2 An *epic* is a long narrative poem which tells of the events or exploits of an heroic person (or persons). In what ways could this poem be considered an epic?

Limbo

And limbo stick is the silence in front of me
limbo

limbo
limbo like me
limbo
limbo like me

long dark night is the silence in front of me
limbo
limbo like me

stick hit sound
and the ship like it ready

stick hit sound
and the dark still steady

limbo
limbo like me

long dark deck and the water surrounding me
long dark deck and the silence is over me

limbo
limbo like me

stick is the whip
and the dark deck is slavery

stick is the whip
and the dark deck is slavery

limbo
limbo like me

drum stick knock
and the darkness is over me

knees spread wide
and the water is hiding

limbo
limbo like me

knees spread wide
and the dark ground is under me

down
down
down

and the drummer is calling me

limbo
limbo like me

sun coming up
and the drummers are praising me

out of the dark
and the dumb gods are raising me

up
up
up

and the music is saving me

hot
slow
step

on the burning ground.

Edward Kamau Brathwaite

Note: It is believed that the limbo dance was devised as a form of exercise on slave ships where conditions below deck were very cramped.

Discussion

Make sure you have read the *note* above. Your teacher or a student will read the poem aloud several times with as much emphasis and feeling as possible. This is an imaginative listening exercise so make a note between readings of any impressions, thoughts or ideas that occur to you.

1 As the poem was read aloud did you enjoy the sound (and mental picture) in such lines as: 'long dark deck and the water surrounding me'? Which other lines did you enjoy and why?
2 What is the effect of the chant of *'limbo'* and *'limbo like me'* throughout the poem?
3 What is the setting for the poem?
4 Is there a reason for the *shape* of the poem?

Written work

Here is a description of the way slaves were treated on their journey across the Atlantic to the West Indies.

The slaves were shackled together by twos, with their hands and feet joined. Some were chained to the deck by the neck and legs. They were given barely enough room to lie down, sit up, or turn around. These positions were sometimes kept for the entire six-to-ten week journey. Air was foul and people died of suffocation. Diseases such as tuberculosis, dysentery, small pox and flux (an abnormal flow of liquid from the body, especially excrement) were common on board. Slaves went mad; many died. Their bodies were thrown into the sea. Sharks often followed ships all the way across the Atlantic.

Use the above passage and the poem for information to enable you to write your own poem or story about a slave voyage from Africa to the West Indies.

Schooner

A tossed night between us
high seas
and then in the morning
sails slack
rope flapping the rigging
your schooner came in

on the deck, buttressed
with mango boxes, chicken-
coops, rice: I saw you:
older than I would wish you
more tattered than my pride
could stand

you saw me
moving reluctant to the quay-
side, stiff as you knew me
too full of pride.
but you had travelled
braved the big wave
and the bilge-swishing stomach,
climbed the tall seas
to come to me

ship was too early
or was I too late?

walking still slowly
(too late or too early?)
saw you suddenly turn
ropes quickly cast off from the capstan
frilled sails were unfurled
water already between your hull and the harbour

too late too late
or too early?

running now
one last rope stretched
to the dockside
tripping over a chain –
chink in my armour –
but the white bows were turning
stern coming round squat in the water

and I
older now
more torn and tattered than my pride
could stand
stretch out my love to you across the water
but cannot reach your hand

Edward Kamau Brathwaite

Discussion

1 Is there a line of thought running through the stanzas? If so, what is it?
2 Is this poem about a writer missing a ship or is it about a quarrel and broken love? Give reasons for your opinion.

Written work

1 From evidence in the poem, build up a character sketch of the speaker.
2 Trace the sea images throughout the poem. Have these images helped you to understand more clearly what the narrator is trying to say? How?

Earth is Brown

Earth is brown and rice is green,
And air is cold on the face of the soul

Oh grandfather, my grandfather,
your dhoti is become a shroud
your straight hair a curse
in this land where
rice no longer fills the belly
or the empty placelessness
of your soul.

For you cannot remember India.
The passage of time
has too long been trampled over
to bear your wistful recollections,
and you only know the name
of the ship they brought you on
because your daadi told it to you.

Your sons with their city faces
don't know it at all
don't want to know it.
Nor to understand that
you cannot cease
this communion with the smell
of cow-dung at fore-day morning,
or the rustling wail
of yellow-green rice
or the security of
mud between your toes
or the sensual pouring
of paddy through your fingers.

Oh grandfather, my grandfather,

your dhoti is become a shroud.
Rice beds no longer call your sons.
They are clerks in the city of streets
where life is a weekly paypacket
purchasing identity in Tiger Bay,
seeking a tomorrow in today's unreality.

You are too old now to doubt
that Hannuman hears you.
Yet outside your logie
the fluttering cane
flaps like a plaintive tabla
in the wind.
And when the spaces inside you
can no longer be filled
by the rank beds of rice,
and the lowing morning
cannot stir you to rise
from your ghoola,
the music in your heart
will sound a rustling sound,
and the bamboos to Hannuman
will be a sitar in the wind.

Shana Yardan

dhoti: loin cloth

shroud: burial garment. This poem is a lament for the poet's grandfather, whose death made her feel that part of the Indian culture in the Caribbean was passing away

Hannuman: Hindu monkey-god noted for his devotion to Rama

tabla: a high pitched, beautiful drum

logie: hut

ghoola: bed

sitar: an Indian lute with a long neck and a varying number of strings

Discussion

1 Why has the title *Earth is Brown* been given to the poem?
2 What is grandfather's daily communion that can be found not only in India but also in the Carribbean?
3 What is your impression of the grandfather?
4 The poet says that the sons have left the reality of the soil for today's 'unreality'. What do you understand that unreality to be?
5 What does this poem tell you about the narrator? What does the narrator feel about the changes that have taken place?

Written work

1 Throughout this poem, there is a sense that times have changed, and that the change has brought a gulf between the grandfather and his children. Explain these changes and how they have separated the generations.
2 Show how the imagery and elements of beauty drawn from the Indian tradition have become part of this poem and also a part of life in the Caribbean.

Love after Love

The time will come
when, with elation,
you will greet yourself arriving
at your own door, in your own mirror,
and each will smile at the other's welcome,

and say sit here. Eat.
You will love again the stranger who was your self.
Give wine. Give bread. Give back your heart
to itself, to the stranger who has loved you

all your life, whom you ignored
for another, who knows you by heart.
Take down the love-letters from the bookshelf

the photographs, the desperate notes,
peel your own images from the mirror.
Sit. Feast on your life.

Derek Walcott

Discussion

1 Explain the title. Which love will return after a love affair is over?
2 How does the poet describe the return of that love?
3 What clearing up process should take place once the love affair is over?

Written work

1 In *Islands*, another poem by Derek Walcott, the poet gave an idea of the kind of poetry he would like to write:

> I seek
> As climate seeks its style, to write
> Verse crisp as sand, clear as sunlight
> Cold as the curved wave, ordinary
> As a tumbler of island water.

How far has he achieved this in *Love after Love*?

2 Try to write the kind of poetry Derek Walcott aspired to. Use this photograph of a woman harvesting rice as the theme of your poem.

Endings

Things do not explode
they fail, they fade,

as sunlight fades from the flesh
as the foam drains quick in the sand,

even love's lightning flash
has no thunderous end,

it dies with the sound
of flowers fading like the flesh

from sweating pumice stone
everything shapes this

till we are left
with the silence that surrounds Beethoven's head.

Derek Walcott

Discussion

1 Look up the definition of *alliteration* in the glossary on page 186. How has alliteration been used in this poem? What effect does this have when the poem is read aloud?

2 Explain the last line of the poem in your own words.

Written work

T. S. Eliot's poem *The Hollow Men* has this nursery rhyme jingle as its last stanza:

This is the way the world ends
This is the way the world ends
This is the way the world ends
Not with a bang but a whimper.

Does Walcott's poem have the same point of view of life? What is that view? Refer in detail to the poem in your answer.

Dark August

So much rain, so much life like the swollen sky
of this black August. My sister, the sun,
broods in her yellow room and won't come out.

Everything goes to hell; the mountains fume
like a kettle, rivers over-run, still,
she will not rise and turn off the rain.

She's in her room, fondling old things,
my poems, turning her album. Even if thunder falls
like a crash of plates from the sky,

she does not come out.
Don't you know I love you but am hopeless
at fixing the rain? But I am learning slowly

to love the dark days, the steaming hills,
the air with gossiping mosquitoes,
and to sip the medicine of bitterness,

so that when you emerge, my sister,
parting the beads of the rain,
with your forehead of flowers and eyes of forgiveness,

all will not be as it was, but it will be true,
(you see they will not let me love
as I want), because my sister, then

I would have learnt to love black days like bright ones,
the black rain, the white hills, when once
I loved only my happiness and you.

Derek Walcott

Discussion

1 Give examples of *personification* in this poem.
2 Why is the poem called *Dark August*? What other title might you give this poem?

Written work

1 On one level this poem is about the author learning to love 'dark August days'. What might his message be on a deeper level?
2 What picture of the poet have you built up from this and the previous two poems?

No Dialects Please

In this competition
dey was lookin for poetry of worth
for a writin that could wrap up a feelin
an fling it back hard
with a captive power to choke de stars
so dey say,
'Send them to us
but NO DIALECTS PLEASE'
We're British!

Ay!
Well ah laugh till me boushet near drop
Is not only dat ah tink

of de dialect of de Normans and de Saxons
dat combine an reformulate
to create a language-elect
is not only dat ah tink
how dis British education mus really be narrow
if it leave dem wid no knowledge
of what dey own history is about
is not only dat ah tink
bout de part of my story
dat come from Liverpool in a big dirty white ship
mark .
AFRICAN SLAVES PLEASE!
We're the British!

But as if dat not enough pain
for a body to bear
ah tink bout de part on de plantations down dere
Wey dey so frighten o de power
in the deep spaces
behind our watching faces
dat dey shout
NO AFRICAN LANGUAGES PLEASE!
It's against the law!

Make me ha to go
an start up a language o me own
dat ah could share wid me people

Den when we start to shout
bout a culture o we own
a language o we own
a identity o we own
dem an de others dey leave to control us say
STOP THAT NONSENSE NOW
We're all British!
Every time we lif we foot to do we own ting

to fight we own fight
dey tell us how British we British
an ah wonder if dey remember
dat in Trinidad in the thirties
dey jail Butler
who dey say is their British citizen
an accuse him of
Hampering the war effort!
Then it was
FIGHT FOR YOUR COUNTRY, FOLKS!
You're British!

Ay! Ay!
Ah wonder when it change to
NO DIALECTS PLEASE!
WE'RE British!
Huh!
To tink how still dey so dunce
an so frighten o we power
dat dey have to hide behind a language
that we could wrap roun we little finger
in addition to we own!
Heavens o mercy!
Dat is dunceness oui!
Ah wonder where is de bright British?

Merle Collins

Discussion

Read through the poem and work out the meaning in standard English.
How does the poem change with the loss of the dialect? Are there any
lines that cannot be changed without losing meaning? Explain why.

Written work

What unfairness is being explained in this poem? Why has the poet used
dialect to explain it?

Shipmates

I watched him as he entered
watched how he sat there
hands deep in pockets
face clenched in total black defiance
eyes moving now from nothing
to rove in angry unconcern
watched how the lips relaxed
just barely
when his eyes passed my face
returned
relaxed
wondered if to recognise perhaps
with cautious smile
moved again
with the easy coldness
born of lifelong practice
born of practical experience

but face not quite so clenched now
for silently he had recognised
another passenger whose averted eyes
could not possibly mean
offence at errant blackness

and as I recognised and shared his pain
my mind wandered
to his history
to our struggles
to our beauty
to our pain

and loving him
I wondered
wondered so hard that when I looked up

the giant hand was pulling to the doors
as the train left my station-stop
wondered
went one stop further
travelled back with clenched faces
black and white
wondered
found no sudden answers
and wandered wonder home

Merle Collins

Discussion

1 What is the setting for this poem?
2 How has the poet's use of alliteration added to the beauty of the sound of this poem?
3 What does the narrator 'share' with her fellow passenger?
4 What picture of Merle Collins have you built up from the two poems in this anthology?

Written work

Explain why this title was chosen for this poem. You may find it useful to look back to pages 155–157 (*Limbo* and the extract on slavery).

Waterpot

The daily going out
and coming in
always being hurried
along
like like...cattle

In the evenings
returning from the fields
she tried hard to walk
like a woman

she tried very hard
pulling herself erect
with every three or four
steps
pulling herself together
holding herself like
royal cane

And the overseer
hurrying them along
in the quickening darkness

And the overseer sneering
them along in the quickening
darkness

sneered at the pathetic –
the pathetic display
of dignity

O but look
there's a waterpot growing
from her head

Grace Nichols

Discussion

1 What do you think is the setting and time of this poem?
2 Why does the person in the poem try hard to 'walk like a woman'? What difference would that make?
3 What kind of man is the overseer?
4 How should the last stanza be read? How has the mood shifted in this last stanza?

Written work

'This poem is about both slavery and freedom.' Agree or disagree.

Two Old Black Men on a Leicester Square Park Bench

What do you dream of you
old black men sitting
on park benches staunchly
wrapped up in scarves
and coats of silence
eyes far away from the cold
grey and strutting
pigeon
ashy fingers trembling
(though it's said that the old
hardly ever feel the cold)

do you dream revolutions
you could have forged
or mourn
some sunfull woman you
might have known a
hibiscus flower
ghost memories of desire

O it's easy
to rainbow the past
after all the letters from
home spoke of hardships

and the sun was traded long ago

Grace Nichols

Discussion

1 From whose point of view is the poem written?
2 Imagine that you are the poet. Describe the thoughts that made you write this poem.
3 What have the old men 'traded' (last line)?
4 Why has the poet deliberately chosen a 'cold' setting?

Written work

It is a summer evening and you are an old person sitting on a park bench. Write a poem in which you begin to remember...

Coursework suggestions

Oral coursework

1 Script and produce a radio programme using some of the poems in this book. You could select poems from one region or poems on a particular theme. Give readings of the poems and provide back-up commentary on the poems themselves and on the authors. You could make a tape or present your programme to a class or group.
2 Organise a rehearsed poetry reading. Select a number of poems and decide how many voices are needed to produce the best effect. Some poems may call for a single voice, others may benefit from using either a number of individual voices or some choral reading – or both. Choose poems that make an interesting blend both of poetry and of presentation.
3 Pick an author whose work appeals to you and find out more about both author and poetry. Prepare a talk which includes poems not printed in this book, as well as your comments on them. If possible, it would help your audience if you could provide copies of any further poems you are introducing.
4 Arrange a meeting with someone who has lived in one of the five regions represented in this book. Interview this person about the kinds of books and poems which he or she remembers coming across or reading while living there. Work out your questions beforehand so that you have a clear idea of what you want to know. You may further wish to write up this interview and point out similarities or differences between the impressions of your interviewee and the impression you have gained from the selection in this book.

Written coursework

1 Pick a topic which interests you and look at how at least three different poets have treated it. Some possible topics include war, poverty, nature, racial tension, aspects of work, politics, the role of women – you may be able to think of others. It is up to you whether you choose your three poems from one section of the book or from more than one. Comment on how the author presents the topic, how he or she leads the reader to some conclusion, how he or she uses language. How do you react to each of these poems?

2 Use any of the sections in this anthology to make a small book of poems on a theme of your choice. Write an introduction to the book and add detailed comments about points in the poems you would like a reader to understand.

3 Under the title 'Past and Present' describe some of the differences between the poems of ancient China, India or Africa, and those of the twentieth century.

4 Write a review of this book. Comment on the choice of poems, drawing attention to any which you found particularly striking; the way the book is organised; the presentation; and the content. What do you think of the book as a resource for English work? What do you think of it as an anthology of poetry for leisure reading? What improvements can you suggest?

5 Pick one of the five regions represented in this book. Write an essay outlining what you have learned about poetry in that region. Do you find any elements that most of the poems have in common? Do you notice any striking differences between the poetry you have studied from this area and any British poetry with which you are familiar?

6 Compare two poets whose beliefs have led them into trouble. How do their poems reflect this trouble? Explain what it is about their poetry which might cause offence to someone.

7 Compare and contrast the poet's handling of a similar theme in any three poems in this book. You may choose poems by the same author or by more than one.

8 Write a report of a group discussion of one or more poems. Make sure you report fairly what other people said, even if you don't agree with it. Include a summary of the conclusions reached by the group and also include your own opinion.

9 Study the work and lives of two poets in this collection who have interested and impressed you. Write up your findings and comment on them.

10 Write your own poetry, using one or more of the poems in this book as a starting point. You may wish to take up a topic from these poems, or model your poems on a style of writing you have encountered here. Make a collection of shorter poems, or write one or two longer ones.

About the poets

Chinese Poetry

The Book of Songs (Shih Ching)   An anthology of poems that were being sung over two thousand years ago, in the fields, houses and palaces of China. The language is simple and apparently close to the daily speech of ordinary people of that time. The themes of the poems are: love, music, farming, war, feasting, hunting and the praise of ancestors.

Chuang Tzu (369–286 BC)   Little is known of Chuang Tzu's life and he may not have written all of *The Chuang Tzu*, the book that bears his name. In this book, the writer gives his view of life and the way it should be lived. This was done by using jokes, stories and parables. The book had a great influence on Chinese painting, poetry and the Buddhist religion.

Lao Tzu (604–523 BC)   Lao Tsu is thought to be the writer of the poems that make up the *Tao Te Ching* (The Way and its Power). Taoism, one of the main religions of China, was based on this book. The *Tao Te Ching* has had a great influence on Chinese philosophy, and in the West has been translated more often than any work except the Bible.

Li Po or *Rihaku* (701–762)   Li Po is regarded as one of China's most important poets. His poems sing about wine, friendship and the passing of time. They are written with great freshness of imagination and a deep sensitivity to the beauties of the language.

Tu Fu (712–770)   At the age of fifteen Tu Fu was already known as a poet with promise. Today he is regarded as one of China's greatest poets. His early poems were about nature and his own personal sorrow, but later he wrote bitingly about war and the contrast of the life of the poor with the richness and splendour of that lived by the emperors.

Po Chü-I (772–846)   Po Chü-I's poems are noted for their deliberate simplicity. This simplicity of style may have made them better subjects for translation, and this may account for the popularity of his poems in Europe and Japan today.

Li Ch'ing-Ch'ao (1081–1150?)   Li Ch'ing-Ch'ao is regarded as China's greatest woman poet. She was a writer of lyric poems to be sung to existing tunes. Her work is noted for its striking use of words and her understanding of emotions. Many of her poems deal with her feelings of sorrow and loneliness after the death of her husband.

Wen Yi-Tuo (1898–1946)   Wen Yi-Tuo was educated in China but studied painting in New York. On his return to China, he worked on ancient Chinese writing, seeking to throw light on the political problems of his day by studying the past.

He came to believe that the entire social and political order had to change before things improved in his country. He protested against the Kuomintang government and was murdered by its soldiers on 15 July 1946.

Kuo Mo-Jo   Kuo Mo-Jo was born in China but spent part of his life in Japan where he wrote poetry and translated works of European literature. When the People's Republic was established, he returned to China and was appointed Vice Premier. He has remained a top leader in the cultural affairs of China ever since.

Yüan Shui-P'ai   Yüan Shui-P'ai's poems were published in Hong Kong at the end of the Second World War. In them he made sharp observations about the awful events that were going on in China at that time. Many of his verses were based on events where people's behaviour differed from what would commonly be considered 'reasonable'.

Indian Poetry

Okkūr Mācātti   Okkūr Mācātti was one of the poets anthologised in *Kuruntokai*. There is evidence in the anthology that Okkūr Mācātti was a woman but little is known about her.

Sir Rabindranath Tagore (1861–1941)   Rabindranath Tagore was born in Calcutta and educated in England. At an early age, he became known internationally for his writing. In 1913 he became the first Indian to receive the Nobel Prize for literature and two years later he was knighted. He resigned his knighthood in 1929 as a protest against British policies in India. The best of his work can be found in *A Tagore Reader*.

Aurobindo Ghose (1872–1950)   Aurobindo Ghose was born in Bhagalpur and educated in England. His poetry was much influenced by science and is deeply concerned with the meaning of existence. He was sent to prison in India for his political activities and on his release he retired to a life apart from others in a search for spiritual truth and experience.

Sarojini Naidu (1879–1950)   Sarojini Naidu was active in the women's movement in India and worked with Gandhi in his fight for freedom. She became a powerful politician and was sent to prison as a result. As a poet she had an eye for description and the finest ear among Indian poets for the sound of English.

A. K. Ramanujan (b.1929)   A. K. Ramanujan spent the first thirty years of his life in India, but he now lives in Chicago. His poetry is about Indian myths and history, the environment, folklore and his family. He has also translated love poems from the *Kuruntokai* (see page 42) and other classic Indian literature.

Shiv K. Kumar (b. 1921)   Shiv K. Kumar's output includes two novels, a play, a short story collection and five volumes of poetry. His poems are concerned with the problems of modern urban living, birth and death, love and companionship.

Nissim Ezekiel (b.1924)   Born in Bombay, Nissim Ezekiel is now Professor of English at Bombay University.

Jayant Mahapatra (b.1928)   Jayant Mahapatra was born in Cuttack and educated at Patna University. His last collection of verse, *Relationships*, won him the Sahitya Akademi Award.

Kamala Das (b.1934)   Kamala Das was born in Malabar. She won early recognition with her many books of short stories and in 1963 she received the PEN Poetry Award (Asian Award). Her poetry is to some extent autobiographical and con-fessional. She has been likened to Sylvia Plath and Anne Sexton.

Dom Moraes (b.1938)   Dom Moraes was born in Bombay. His father was the editor of the *India Express*. At the age of fifteen he came to England and was later educated at Oxford University. In 1958 he won the Hawthornden Prize for poetry. He is one of the best-known Indian poets writing in English.

Debjani Chatterjee   Debjani Chatterjee was born in Delhi but came to England with her parents after the partition of India and Pakistan in 1947. Her writing is not confined to poetry for she is also the author of *The Role of Religion in A Passage to India*.

Pakistani Poetry

Sir Mohammed Iqbāl (1876–1938)   Mohammed Iqbāl is now regarded as Pakistan's national poet. He was born in Sialkot in the Punjab. He was one of the earliest believers in a separate Muslim state and many of his ideas helped in the formation of Pakistan. In 1924 he accepted a knighthood. Some of his best poems are con-tained in *Gabriel's Wing*.

Faiz Ahmad Faiz (1911–1984)   Faiz Ahmad Faiz was also born in Sialkot. As a com-munist, he was popular in Russia where all his poems have been translated. Some of his poems are about prison, where he was sent several times by the Pakistani government. One of his best collections in English is *Poems by Faiz* (1971).

Nazir Ahmad Shaikh   Nazir Ahmad Shaikh takes a humorous view in his poetry of natural and man-made disasters and misfortunes. The content of his poetry ranges widely: the black market, the plight of refugees, the overcrowded and dilapidated buses, the chaotic railway stations, the floods, and disasters in general.

Shahid Hosain (b.1934)   Shahid Hosain was born in Aligarh and now lives and works in Lahore. His poetry has been published in American magazines and in *First Voices* (1969).

Taufiq Rafat (b.1927)   Taufiq Rafat was born in Sialkot and still lives there today. He has been writing poetry since the age of twelve and it has appeared in magazines in America, Australia and in English anthologies. He is also the author of a full-length play in English.

M. K. Hameed   M. K. Hameed has had poems published in American, Canadian and British magazines. His work has also been included in two anthologies, *Young Commonwealth Poets* and *New Voices of the Commonwealth*.

Zulfikar Ghose (b.1935)   Zulfikar Ghose was born in Sialkot but he came to England when he was seventeen and studied at Keele University. A number of his poems tell of memories of childhood and family life. His collection *Jets from Orange* was published in 1968.

Adrian Hussain (b. 1942)   Adrian Hussain was born in Kanpur, but he was educated at schools in England and Europe and then went to New College, Oxford. He began writing poetry while still at school and since then has had a number of his poems published in English magazines.

African Poetry

Léopold Sédar Senghor (1906–1988)   Léopold Senghor was born at Joal near Dakar. He was educated locally and then at the Sorbonne, Paris. While at the Sorbonne, he met the Martinique poet Aime Cesaire and together they worked out the literary idea known as *negritude*, which sought to uphold African culture and values against those of the hostile white world. In 1955 Senghor became a minister in the French government and in 1960 he was elected the first president of the Republic of Senegal.

Agostinho Neto (1922–1980)   Agostinho Neto was born in Portuguese West Africa. He studied medicine in Portugal and returned to Angola to practise. He joined a revolutionary group and was arrested four times before being sent to jail in Portugal. In 1962 he escaped and became leader of the struggle against colonial rule. When Angola became independent he was made president. His poetry was concerned with political and social unrest.

Chinua Achebe (b.1930)   Chinua Achebe was born in Nigeria. He is best known as a novelist but has published several collections of short stories and a volume of poetry. Among the many honours he has received was a nomination for the Nobel Prize for Literature.

Okot p'Bitek (1931–1982)   Okot p'Bitek was born in Uganda and received his secondary education there. He attended universities in England and on his return to Uganda became director of the National Theatre. Among his published books are three volumes of poetry, a collection of Acholi poetry and a collection of Acholi folktales (he was a member of the Acholi tribe).

Lenrie Peters (b.1932)   Lenrie Peters was born in Gambia and was educated there and in England where he studied medicine. He has taken part in BBC programmes dealing with African literature and has written a novel and two volumes of poetry.

John Pepper Clark (b.1935) John Pepper Clark was born in Nigeria. He started work as a journalist but is now a lecturer at Lagos University. He has published three collections of poetry and written three plays. His poetry has been very well received and he is regarded by many to be one of Africa's best poets.

Joyce Nomafa Sikakane Joyce Sikakane is South African. Her poem, *An Agony* first appeared in *The Classic* magazine.

Susan Lwanga Born in Uganda, she has published poems in the East African magazine *Pulsations*.

Yambo Ouologuem (b.1940) Yambo Ouologuem was born in Mali. He studied in Paris and it was there that he published *Bound to Violence*, a novel that won him the Prix Renaudot. Many of his poems have been published in magazines and anthologies.

Oswald Mbuyiseni Mtshali (b.1940) Oswald Mtshali was born in Natal in South Africa. His only volume of poems, *Sounds of a Cowhide Drum* was published in 1971. It contained poems of black awareness and experience which brought him to the attention of the authorities who placed him under house arrest.

Jack Mapanje (b. 1946) Jack Mapanje is a leading black African poet from Malawi. He is well-known as an expert in African oral literature and edits *Kalulu*, a magazine devoted to that. He has published a volume of his own poems under the title *Of Chameleons and Gods*. At the moment the security police in Malawi are holding him as a prisoner without the right to speak to anyone.

Musaemura Bonas Zimunya Musaemura Zimunya was born in Zimbabwe. He took part in the struggle to liberate his country and was jailed by the white minority government. He was very much a part of the awakening of African literature at that time. His collection of poems, *Thought-Tracks* was published in 1982.

Caribbean Poetry

Philip Sherlock (b. 1902) Philip Sherlock was born in Jamaica. He became a publisher of books in 1936 and these include an anthology of poetry for West Indian schools, several collections of folk tales and a number of Caribbean readers. He was knighted in 1967. His poetry was an important contribution to the literary re-birth of Caribbean poetry in the 1940s and 1950s.

Martin Carter (b.1927) Martin Carter was born in Georgetown, Guyana. He was active in the nationalist movement and was sent to prison in 1953. In 1965 he was Guyana's representative at the Commonwealth Poetry Conference in Cardiff and later became Minister of Public Information and Broadcasting for the Guyanese Government.

Dennis Scott (b.1939) Dennis Scott was born in Kingston, Jamaica. His poetry has brought him several national prizes and one collection, *Uncle Time*, was winner of the International Poetry Forum Award and Commonwealth Poetry Prize.

Lorna Goodison (b.1947)   Lorna Goodison was born in Jamaica and educated both there and in New York. Her first collection of poetry was entitled *Tamarind Season* and both this and her subsequent poetry have been praised by the critics. She is also an artist who has exhibited in Jamaica and Guyana, and *Tamarind Season* is illustrated by her.

Edward Kamau Brathwaite (b.1930)   Edward Brathwaite was born in Bridgetown, Barbados. Although first and foremost a Caribbean writer, he is recognised as a major world poet writing in English. He has received many awards for his poetry including an Arts Council of Great Britain Poetry Bursary. His best known verse comes from *The Arrivants* and *X/Self*.

Shana Yardan   Shana Yardan was born in Guyana of Indian descent and often writes about her Indian relatives and ancestors. Poems by her can be found in *A Treasury of Guyanese Poetry* edited by A. J. Seymour.

Derek Walcott (b.1930)   Derek Walcott was born in Castries, St Lucia and is a poet with an international reputation. He has received many awards for his poetry including the Royal Society of Literature Award. His best-known verse comes from *Collected Poems: 1948–1984* and *The Arkansas Testament*.

Merle Collins   Merle Collins was born and grew up in Grenada. She left Grenada when the United States invaded it in 1983 and ousted the marxist regime. She is a member of 'African Dawn', a group that performs dramatised poetry with African music.

Grace Nichols (b.1950)   Grace Nichols was born in Guyana but came to Britain in 1977. In 1983 she received the Commonwealth Poetry Prize for her collection *i is a long memoried woman*.

Glossary

Alliteration: The repetition of the same initial letter, or initial vowel sounds, in two or more consecutive or nearly consecutive words, e.g.
Letter alliteration:

> Fling *forth furled flags*, and let them play
> Thrill all hearts this victorious day.

Vowel alliteration:

> I watch the green field *growing*
> For reaping folk and *sowing*,
> For harvest-time and *mowing*,
>   A sleepy world of streams.

Assonance: The repeating of vowel sounds in the words of a line of poetry, e.g.

> d*ee*p and dr*ea*mless sl*ee*p

Ballad: A narrative poem, usually fairly short and originally designed to be sung.
Descriptive poem: One that gives a vivid impression of a person or a scene.
Epic: A long poem which tells the story of an event, or a series of events, whether historical or imaginative, concerning heroic action by one or more people, usually over a long period of time.
Epistle: Poetry composed in the form of a letter.
Figure of speech: A word or phrase used for vivid or dramatic effect and not literally. The most common figures of speech in poetry are simile, metaphor and personification.
Form: The organisation of a poem; its structure, metres and stanzas.
Free verse: Verse released from the convention of metre, with its regular pattern of stresses and line lengths.
Hyperbole: Exaggeration for effect: e.g. I have a stack of work about a mile high.
Irony: Use of language to convey a meaning opposite to that literally stated and which aims at ridicule or humour: e.g. Ray and Steve are a couple of bright specimens.
Lyric: In ancient times, poetry that was sung to the tune of a lute. Now, the kind of poetry that describes the poet's own feelings and thoughts, e.g.

> Love is a sickness full of woes,
>   All remedies refusing;
> A plant that with most cutting grows,
>   Most barren with best using.
>   Why so?

Metre: The rhythm of lines of poetry. This rhythm depends on the emphasis given to certain syllables when spoken aloud. The arrangement of these accents or stresses in the form of a regular pattern is called metre.

Metaphor: A description of something in terms of something else without using *like* or *as*, e.g. No man *is* an island, entire of itself.

Mood: The tone, e.g. thoughtful, sad, funny, which is used most of the time in a stanza or poem.

Narrative poem: Poetry which tells a story. There is no particular form, although it may contain lyrical or descriptive passages.

Onomatopoeia: The imitation of the sound of a thing by the use of words or impressions, e.g. The murmuring of innumerable bees.

Parody: An imitation of the style of a poem or other literary work for fun or ridicule.

Pathos: That which arouses feelings of pity, sympathy or sadness.

Personification: A form of metaphor in which things are referred to as if they were human beings, e.g.

> The joyous morning ran and kissed the grass,
> And drew his fingers through her sleeping hair.

Reflective poem: One that expresses the writer's serious thoughts on some matter he or she thinks important.

Rhyme: A word that rhymes with another, e.g. You can rhyme *bustard* with *mustard* and *custard* but not with *mural*, *plural* and *rural*. Words that rhyme at the ends of lines in poetry have a pattern. One of the most common patterns is the A B A B A, e.g.

> I wandered lonely as a cloud   A
> That floats on high o'er vales and hills B
> When all at once I saw a crowd   A
> A host, of golden daffodils;   B

Ear rhymes are those that rhyme according to the ear rather than the eye, e.g.

> Nothing save the airs that *brood*
> Over the magic *solitude.*

Eye rhymes are spelled similarly but pronounced differently, e.g.

> Teach me to hear mermaids singing,
> Or to keep off envy's stinging,
>   And *find*
>   What *wind*
> Serves to advance an honest *mind.*

Rhythm: Another name for metre, a regular pattern of beats, the music of poetry, e.g.

> The Assyrian came down like the wolf on the fold,
> And his cohorts were gleaming in purple and gold;
> And the sheen of their spears was like stars on the sea
> When the blue wave rolls nightly on deep Galilee.

Satire: Literature which examines vice and folly and makes them appear ridiculous or contemptible.

Simile: Saying that one thing is like another using *like* or *as*, e.g.

> He stood there in the road
> *Like* Roland's ghost winding a silent horn.

> The house was *as* still as death now.

Stanza: A group of lines of poetry that belong together. It is set off from other stanzas by an extra space between the last line of one stanza and the first line of the next.

Acknowledgements

We wish to thank Robyn Alton and Margaret Mackey for their consultations during the writing of this book.

We are grateful to the following for permission to reproduce copyright material:

Jonathan Cape Ltd for the poems 'Love After Love', 'Endings' & 'Dark August' in *Sea Grapes* by Derek Walcott; Century Hutchinson Publishing Group Ltd for an extract from *Tongues of Men* by V Crellin; the author, Debjani Chatterjee for her poem 'I was that woman' in *Watchers & Seekers* ed by R Cobham & M Collins (Women's Press, 1987); the author, Merle Collins for her poems 'Shipmates' & 'No Dialects Please' in *Watchers & Seekers* ed by R Cobham & M Collins (Women's Press, 1987). Copyright Merle Collins; Constable & Co Ltd for the poem 'The Red Cockatoo' by Po Chü-I in *170 Chinese Poems* trans by Arthur Waley; the author, Kamala Das for her poems 'An Introduction' & 'The House-Builders'; Doubleday, a Division of Bantam, Doubleday, Dell Publishing Group, Inc, for extracts from poems in *Twentieth Century Chinese Poetry* trans by Kai-Yu Hsu. Copyright (c) 1963 by Kai-Yu Hsu; the author, Nissim Ezekiel & Oxford University Press, India, for the poems 'Poverty Poems – 2' in *Collected*

Poems by Nissim Ezekiel & 'Night of the Scorpion' in *Latter Day Psalms* by Nissim Ezekiel, first published in *The Exact Name* (Writer's Workshop, 1966); Faber & Faber Ltd for the poem 'Taking Leave of a Friend' by Rihaku in *Collected Shorter Poems* by Ezra Pound; the author, Zulfikar Ghose for his poem 'A Note on the Existence of God' in *The Loss of India* (pub Routledge & Kegan Paul, 1964); the author's agent for the poems 'The Picnic in Jammu' by Zulfikar Ghose, copyright (c) 1967 by Zulfikar Ghose, first published in *Jets From Orange* (Macmillan London) & 'In the Desert' by Zulfikar Ghose, copyright (c) 1972 by Zulfikar Ghose, first published in *The Violent West* (Macmillan London); the author, Lorna Goodison for her poem 'For My Mother'; Gower Publishing Company Ltd for the poems 'Truthful Words Are Not Beautiful' & 'Fame or Self' by Lao Tzu in *Tao Te Ching* trans by Gia-Fu Feng & Jane English; Heinemann Educational Books Ltd for the poems 'Refugee Mother & Child' & 'Vultures' in *Beware Soul Brother* by Chinua Achebe, 'The Sweet Brew at Chitakale' & 'When this Carnival Finally Closes' in *Of Chameleons & Gods* by Jack Mapanje, 'Parachute Men Say' & 'You Talk to Me of Self' in *Selected Poetry* by Lenrie Peters; the author, Shahid Hosain for his poems 'A Speculation' in *First Voices: Six Poets from Pakistan* ed by Shahid Hosain (Oxford University Press, 1969) & 'Across the Indus' in *Pieces of Eight: Eight Poets from Pakistan* ed by Yunus Said (Oxford University Press, 1971); Kenya Literature Bureau for the poem 'Daybreak' by Susan Lwanga in *Pulsations*; Lawrence & Wishart Ltd for the poems 'This is the Dark Time My Love' in *Poems of Resistance* by Martin Carter (1954) & 'Bent' in *Poems of Affinity* by Martin Carter (1954); Longman Group UK Ltd for the poem 'To Mai' in *Thought-Tracks* by Musaemura Bonas Zimunya (Longman Drum-beat Series). Copyright Musaemura Bonas Zimunya; Macmillan, London & Basingstoke, for extracts from *The Collected Poems & Plays of Rabindranath Tagore* by Rabindranath Tagore; the author's agent for the poems 'African Poem' & 'February' in *When Bullets Begin To Flower* by W S Merwin; the author's agents for extracts from the poems 'Gone Away' & 'At Seven O'Clock' in *Poems* by Dom Moraes (Eyre & Spottiswoode, 1960), (c) Dom Moraes; the author, Grace Nichols for her poems 'Waterpot' in *I Is A Long Memoried Woman* (Karnak House, 1983) & 'Two Old Black Men on a Leicester Square Park Bench' in *The Fat Black Woman's Poems* (Virago Press); Peter Owen Ltd for the poems 'Obituary', 'Breaded Fish', 'The Striders', 'What She Said' & 'What her Girlfriend Said to Her' in *The Interior Landscape: Love Poems From A Classical Tamil Anthology* trans by A K Ramanujan; Oxford University Press for the poems 'Limbo' in *The Arrivants* by Edward Kamau Brathwaite (1973), 'Schooner' in *Other Exiles* by Edward Kamau Brathwaite (1975), 'In Praise of a Blacksmith' from

Shona Praise Poetry compiled by Aaron C Hodza, trans by George Fortune (1979), 'Always a Suspect' in *Sounds of a Cowhide Drum* by Mbuyiseni Oswald Mtshali (1971), 'Is It Surprising My Dear' & 'Long, long have you held between your hands' in *Selected Poems* by Léopold Sédar Senghor, trans by John Reed & Clive Wake (1964), (c) Oxford University Press, 1964; Oxford University Press, India, for the poems 'Beyond the Stars' by Mohammed Iqbal & 'Dust Storm' by Nazir Ahmad Shaikh in *A History of Urdu Literature 2nd Edition* trans by Muhammad Sadiq (Oxford University Press, 1984); The Oxford University Press, India, & the author, Jayanta Mahapatra for the poem 'Again, One Day Walking by the River' in *Life Signs* (OUP, 1983), first published in *Kenyon Review*; the author's agent for extracts from poems in *The White Pony* trans by Robert Payne; the author, J P Clark for his poems 'Agbor Dancer's & 'Incident at the Police Station, Warri' in *A Reed in the Tide*; Penguin Books Ltd for extracts from poems in *The Penguin Book of Chinese Verse* trans by Robert Kotewall & Norman L Smith (Penguin Books, 1962), copyright (c) Robert Kotewall & Norman L Smith, 1962, & the poems 'Do not Ask of Me, My Love' & 'Freedom's Dawn' by Faiz Ahmad Faiz in *The Penguin Book of Urdu Poetry* trans by Mahmood Jamal (Penguin Books, 1986), copyright (c) Mahmood Jamal, 1986; Presence Africaine for the poem 'Tomatoes' by Yambo Ouologuem, originally published under the title 'Quand parlent les dents negres' in *Nouvelle Somme De Poesie Du Monde Noir* Presence Africaine, Paris, 1966 (Review No 57); the author, Philip Sherlock for extracts from his poems 'Jamaican Fisherman' & 'Pocomania'; Sidgwick & Jackson Ltd for the poem 'Insomnia' by Shiv K Kumar in *Woodpeckers* (1979); Sterling Publishers Pvt Ltd for the poems 'The Tiger & the Deer' by Sri Aurobindo Ghose, 'Village Song' & 'The Pradah Nashin' by Sarojini Naidu in *Indian Poetry In English* trans by Prasad & Singh; the author's agent for the poems 'The Joy of Fishes' & 'Two Kings & No-Form' in *The Way of Chuang Tzu* by Chuang Tzu (New Directions Publishing Corporation); UNESCO for the poems 'Flows like a Wave of Wine' & 'A Prison Nightfall' by Faiz Ahmad Faiz in *Poems By Faiz*, Unesco Collection of Representative Works, (c) Unesco 1971; University of Pittsburgh Press for the poems 'Uncle Time' & 'Epitaph' in *Uncle Time* by Dennis Scott, (c) 1973 by Dennis Scott; Unwin Hyman Ltd for extracts from poems in *More Translations from the Chinese* trans by Arthur Waley; Urdu Markaz for an extract from the poem 'Address to the Saki' by Mohammed Iqbal in *Urbu Literature* ed by D J Matthews, C Shackle & Shahrukh Hussain.

We have been unable to locate the copyright holders in the following and would appreciate any information that will enable us to do so:

'The Fulani Creation Story' trans from the Zulu by Malam Hampate Ba, first published in *Black Orpheus No. 19*; the poems 'Men In Moonlight' & 'Gold Spot Glow' by M K Hameed in *Pieces of Eight: Eight Poets from Pakistan* ed by Yunus Said (Oxford University Press, 1969); the poems 'Modern Cookery' & 'Modern Girl' by Okot p'Bitek in *Song of Lawino* (East African Publishing House); the poems 'I am glad to be up and about' by Taufiq Rafat in *First Voices: Six Poets from Pakistan* ed by Shahid Hosain (Oxford University Press, 1969) & 'Sacrifice' by Taufiq Rafat in *Pieces of Eight: Eight Poets from Pakistan* ed by Yunus Said (Oxford University Press, 1971); *Appointment in Crete* by A M Rendel (Alan Wingate); the poem 'An Agony' by Joyce Nomafa Sikakane' in *The Return of the Amasi Bird* ed by Couzens & Patel (Ravan Press Pty Ltd); the poem 'Earth is Brown' by Shana Yardan in *A Treasury of Guyanese Poetry* ed A J Seymour (1980); the poem 'Love Song', traditional from the Amharic, translation first published in *Black Orpheus No. 19*; the poem 'The Magnificent Bull', traditional from the Dinka, translation published in *African Poetry for Schools* (East African Publishing House, 1970).

We are grateful to the following for permission to use photographs: Anne Bolt, page 164; J. Allan Cash, pages 97, 141; Bruce Coleman, pages 73 (Michael Freeman), 112 (Werner Layer); James Davis Travel Photography, page 53; Sally & Richard Greenhill, page 41; Hong Kong Tourist Association, page 13; London Zoo, page 25; Werner Forman Archive/ Herbert Rieser Collection, London, page 101.